PREGNANCY GUIDE FOR MEN

How to help during pregnancy, being 100% there for her when you're expecting

VINCENT O.

PREGNANCY GUIDE FOR MEN

How to help during pregnancy, being 100% there for her when you're expecting

Copyright © 2022 by Vincent O.

Printed in the United States of America

CONTENTS

INTRODUCTION

Becoming a dad is a life-altering event, *but how do we describe it?*

> " The only way I can describe fatherhood is at the end of How the Grinch Stole Christmas, you know how his heart grows like five times? Everything is full; it's just full all the time."
>
> — MATT DAMON

It's true! The love you feel when you first become a parent is amazing regardless of whether you're a mother or father-to-be. Until you experience it for yourself, you don't truly understand it. When you first find out that your other half is pregnant, it's likely you'll feel happy, or even surprised. Some of us don't know how we should feel because while we want to be a father and recognize this is a beautiful thing, but we don't really know what to do or what to expect throughout the pregnancy months.

When reality hits, the whole pregnancy process and the idea of becoming a father can be overwhelming!

Pregnancy is typically all about women, and I'm not saying it shouldn't be but as men, we're detached from the situation. For some, it's like we're the third wheel of pregnancy. While a woman goes through morning sickness, and other symptoms of pregnancy as they lead up to the birth, they are the first to feel the baby move and kick. They're already bonding with the baby but the father doesn't get exactly the same experience. It can be difficult to involve ourselves in a supportive way or sense what to do and when to do it.

But this isn't a pity book for fathers though…

You don't need pity, you need guidance and support (even though you probably don't want to admit it). The methods, tips, and tricks discussed in this book will help you overcome any barriers or fears, get more involved in the pregnancy process, and ensure you can confidently support your partner throughout each stage of pregnancy.

Just think how great it would be to know exactly what to do and show up for your partner, confidently, throughout the whole of her pregnancy.

You can do this!

Supporting your partner in the way they need you to, is something you don't always automatically know, especially when we're a first-time father (most of us are not psychic). Sometimes we get things wrong – I know I did, and I am not ashamed to admit it!

The truth is, there are probably things you'll get wrong on this journey too. We're human beings and we're not exempt from making mistakes. We don't always know or understand the emotional and physical changes that happen to women during pregnancy and such changes can be worrying for us. If you want to be able to support your partner in the best way possible, this honest, yet practical book, is exactly what you need, and it will certainly help you get in your partner's good books.

When our partners are going through changes, suffering from symptoms, or heading towards a time of pain during birth, it can be a scary time for the father too. Yet so many of us bottle up how we feel because we don't want to make it worse for our other half. It's okay to feel this way, in fact, it shows we care. We want to take the pain away from our loved ones, but this entire process is beyond our control, and this can stir up feelings of frustration.

While you can't take away the pain for your partner, you can still support them well. This book will help you strengthen your understanding of pregnancy from start to finish, so you know exactly what to do and expect, even if:

- You're unsure of your new responsibilities and need some help and guidance regarding those
- You have no clue about what kind of dad you want to be, or how to be a good dad
- Your father was absent, and you don't want to make the same mistakes

Remember that our past experiences make us who we are, they help us learn and grow, and by showing up here and reading this book, you've already proved your commitment to fatherhood!

I understand the fears of becoming a first-time father as I have first-hand knowledge of this. I've been the nervous partner, not knowing quite what to do or say to my partner during her pregnancy. At the start of her first pregnancy, I didn't know how things worked. We didn't know she was pregnant until she was 6 weeks, but we kept it quiet until we'd had our first ultrasound.

Morning sickness was a nightmare, and I didn't know how to comfort my wife or what would ease her symptoms. Still, she soldiered on and went to work, and when I came home, my dinner was on the table. I did not know if I should offer to cook dinner and encourage her to rest, or if she just wanted to continue as normal… Until I finally asked her (I really don't know why it took me so long to ask).

I worked late a lot, and it turned out she was hungry and low on energy as soon as she got home, so she couldn't wait for me to cook. We came to a compromise. A couple of nights a week, I prepared something suitably nutritious for the next day, so she could oven-bake it when she arrived home. This worked well for us, and obviously, I took care of the dishes once I was home.

I wasn't there for appointments and ultrasounds due to my job, but the first time I felt the baby kick, I was overwhelmed. I had no idea of how big the baby was at that time, or the birthing options available to us, so I started to research the facts. I didn't even realize that I could have time off work following the birth until my boss told me. There was so much I hadn't considered.

This was just the tip of the iceberg – it dawned on me that I had no idea what was going on in my wife's body, or what would ease her aching back and swollen feet as the end of her pregnancy approached and more stress was placed on her body. At first, I felt disappointed in myself because of the things I didn't know, but I soon realized that this was not because I wasn't going to be a great dad, but because I simply didn't know – nobody tells you this stuff!

I knew I had to take control!

In my family, we didn't talk about the ins and outs of pregnancy or other personal stuff, so I had to go and figure it out on my own and I started by exploring what pregnancy brings each week and month at a time. My wife and I now have two children together with another on the way (we haven't officially announced this yet, as we're only into the second month), but each experience taught me something new, and each time I got better.

While every pregnancy and birth are different, I've come to understand what to expect and what I can do to help my partner. That's why I've developed the tips and tricks needed to make the process as seamless as possible, for you and your pregnant partner. I believe it's time to alleviate the nerves and uncertainty for first-time fathers, so they get to enjoy their partner's pregnancy too. *You deserve it!*

This book will look at pregnancy on a month-by-month basis, so you know and understand your baby's development, as well as looking at the signs and symptoms that your partner may be suffering from. We'll start at the beginning, by exploring the first signs of pregnancy and the development of your child. We'll even talk you through your first appointments with healthcare professionals, so you know who you should see and when you should see them, as we move through the different trimesters with your partner.

This book will also provide you with advice and guidance throughout your journey, so you can prepare for each stage and the birth, as well as being the best support you can be.

This means you can fully embrace your inner super-man (before you transition into super-dad)!

Remember…

 Being a great father is like shaving. No matter how good you shaved today, you have to do it again tomorrow."

— REED MARKHAM

THE FIRST MONTH

So, you're going to be a dad…

That's great. But many dad-to-be's aren't sure what even happens in the first month of pregnancy. This chapter covers information that you need to know within the first month, and because it's so easy to get it wrong in the beginning, we'll talk about the normal things you should consider or say when you find out your partner is pregnant. We'll also talk about prenatal appointments and provide you with some helpful tips, to ensure you're well-prepared!

I always remember when my partner uttered the words 'I'm pregnant' for the first time. I don't know whether my face showed happiness, elation, or fear, as it's all kind of hazy, and I remember thinking 'Wow! This is really happening,'. Even though it was planned, I didn't know how to react.

Some people may not understand ovulation, how conception works, and what to do (or not) if they are trying to conceive. We'll cover all the things I wish someone had told me in the beginning, to prevent me from feeling completely clueless.

This book has your back, so you no longer need to experience clue-lessness – we're in this together, so let's start with a weird and wonderful fact about early pregnancy.

Incredible Fact #1

Most people don't realize that dads can get pregnancy symptoms and they usually make an appearance towards the end of the first trimester (first 3 months of pregnancy). This is called Couvade Syndrome, but nobody really knows why it happens. While fathers experience sympathy symptoms of pregnancy, it is not a mental health issue, nor a recognized medical condition.

Symptoms of Couvade syndrome include:

- Heartburn
- Leg cramps
- Backpain
- Toothache
- Restlessness
- Nausea
- Stomach pain
- Bloating
- Diarrhea
- Constipation
- Sleep issues
- Changes in weight or appetite
- Urinatory issues
- Genital discomfort
- Libido issues

Generally, symptoms subside or improve within the second trimester (3-6 months), and then they can return in the third trimester (6-9 months). Typically, symptoms disappear after the birth of your baby.

Pregnancy Weeks 1-4

During weeks 1-4, ovulation has just happened, and the expectant mom may not even know she's pregnant yet…

Ovulation is an important part of a woman's menstrual cycle, as this is when an egg is released from the ovary. If the egg is fertilized, this is the very start of a pregnancy which is called conception. The egg then travels to the uterus, through the fallopian tube, and over the next 7 days, the human embryo goes through a process called mitosis. This is a series of cell divisions that transforms the embryo into a mass of organized cells. This is called the blastocyst, and it usually happens on the 12th day of pregnancy. This means that the embryo can burrow deep into the lining of the uterus, by implanting, allowing it to develop further.

There are no signs or symptoms of implantation for most women although some report abdominal cramps, swollen breasts, headaches, low energy, or even light bleeding. For the egg to implant, the uterus and embryo must both be healthy and receptive. Sometimes, the blastocyst implants but does not develop, and if this happens within two weeks, the pregnancy would not be detected. Egg quality also plays a huge part in conception, and this can diminish as a woman ages. 50% of all women's eggs are lost before they get to the blastocyst stage.

A woman would not necessarily know if they pregnant or not at this point of pregnancy. Pregnancy hormones are just starting to develop, which can lead to feelings of tiredness and mood swings. It's a good idea for the expectant mother to eat foods that are high in vitamin C and iron to compensate for this. You'll find iron in beef, spinach, dried fruit and poultry, whereas vitamin C is in foods such as asparagus, melon, strawberries, and tomatoes. Keeping hydrated and ensuring enough calcium is consumed is also important to help the baby develop strong bones and organs. Yogurts, pasteurized cheeses, and milk are good ways to increase your calcium intake. It's certainly a good idea to make healthier food choices when trying to conceive!

By 4 weeks, your baby is the size of a poppy seed. It does not yet have a heartbeat, but the heart is beginning to develop in the form of a blood vessel, however, it will not beat for another week or two. This is a suitable time to find out if you or your partner are pregnant by taking a test, as the closer she gets to her period due date, the more likely she is to get an accurate reading, although early detection is possible.

At this stage, the pregnant woman will not have started to develop a pregnancy stomach yet but could feel bloated at 4 weeks. As the baby is at an important stage of development, it is a good idea for the expectant mom to start taking 400 micrograms of folic acid, every day, as this prevents birth defects.

Normal Things Men Think or Say When Hearing the Words "I'm Pregnant"

When our partner first tells us they're pregnant, we don't always respond in the right way and sometimes we say things we don't mean. A friend of mine had been trying for a baby with his wife for a few months, and when he arrived home from work one evening, his wife told him she was pregnant. *What do you think his response was?*

He asked her "Is it mine?"

He told me he couldn't believe he'd asked such a question and doesn't know why he did. He just didn't know how to respond or how to react to such big news…

Needless to say, it didn't go down well!

It's important to accept that we don't always know what to do or say. Even when a baby is planned, we can start to freak out when reality hits, but in the initial stages, many people decide not to broadcast the news which can be tricky if you're excited about it. Most people have more practical worries, such as money, housing issues, and thoughts of how much their life will change. Sometimes pregnancy isn't planned, which can be extremely overwhelming. If you've split up with your partner, haven't been with them long, or if you're young and didn't plan on this happening so soon, it impacts your response. Other men tend to make jokes to celebrate that conception is successful and others are simply happy that their boys can swim!

If you're in the habit of occasionally saying the wrong thing and aren't sure what you'll say when your other half tells you they are pregnant, don't worry, we've constructed a list below of some appropriate responses:

1. This is great news! – if you're thrilled about the pregnancy, let your partner know. Sometimes they need reassurance that you're happy too. It's good to look at the positives, but make sure you listen to her regardless to ensure it's what you both want. Talk through everything together and plan ahead to build excitement.

2. How are you feeling? – this is always a good response because pregnancy can be tough. It takes its toll on your hormones and your body, so asking how they feel is a good move as it shows you care!

3. What do you want to do? – even if the pregnancy is planned, a woman may feel mixed emotions right now, so it's important to listen to her and talk through any worries she has.

4. What can I do to help? – just knowing you're on hand to help if she needs it can make a difference as it ensures she feels supported and feels able to talk through any concerns. You're there to help, and she can rely on you.

5. We got this! Everything is going to be fine – sometimes, she just needs reassurance. If you're willing to handle it and it's what you both want, you can do it. While it may be overwhelming or exciting at first, you got this, so show your partner unity.

6. I'm here for you – this is a bold, but reassuring statement. While your partner may not need you to do something instantly, just knowing you're there and you have their back can help.

7. We're going to have a great family – letting your partner know you are in it for the long haul and recognizing that it's part of something bigger, in the future, can be a wonderful thing to say to your partner as it helps to build the excitement. Family is the best!

8. You are amazing! – saying something as simple as that can make your partner feel happy and good. Remember, they do not know how you feel about the pregnancy until you react. Pregnancy is an amazing thing, as she is growing a little human that you are both going to take care of.

Planning a response is great if you are in the early stages, or are planning a pregnancy, as sometimes we cannot control our initial response. We can also feel under pressure because we don't know how our other half wants us to respond.

Sometimes, it's unfair to judge what's right or wrong when it comes to these things, and the reality of being pregnant can be scary for all. *Try reflecting on some ways you could respond if you found out that your other half was pregnant.*

Even my friend who asked if the baby was his, came good in the end, but this is certainly a question I'd suggest you avoid asking unless it's an essential question that you need to ask. While they laugh about it now, it killed the positive dialogue!

Prenatal Appointments

At this stage in the pregnancy, there won't be many prenatal appointments as you've just found out you're going to be a parent. If you're trying for a baby, or are having difficulty conceiving, it's certainly worth booking an initial appointment for you and your partner with your doctor about this. If you've just found out you're having a baby and are about 4 weeks, the first appointment should be with the doctor at this stage. Your partner can take you, go alone, or take someone else with them if they wish.

Although you book your appointment at this stage, it may not happen for a few weeks, but that means you've got time to prepare. When you attend your first medical appointment there may be so many things you want to know, so you and your partner should note down a list of questions that you want to ask. This could include:

- Do you recommend any prenatal vitamins?
- When it comes to weight gain, how much weight is healthy for me during pregnancy?
- Am I at risk of any health conditions or complications?
- What medications are safe for me (prescription and over-the-counter)?
- Is exercise safe for me, during pregnancy?
- Can I have sex?
- Are there any foods I should eat or avoid?
- Who should I call if I have any worries, concerns, or questions regarding my pregnancy?
- Are there any prenatal screenings I need to have?

- What symptoms should I have and are there any in particular that I should talk to you about?
- Who delivers my baby and what are the options?
- How can I relieve my pregnancy symptoms?

The Dos and Don'ts of Conceiving

Do…

Track her cycle together – there's a stigma surrounding menstruation, but we can challenge that. If you get involved and embrace the idea, it helps your other half open up. It's always suggested that a woman who is trying to conceive tracks her cycle, *so why can't this involve you too?* It is such an effective way to support your partner and let them know, you are in this together. Talk about this first to check she's comfortable with this – you don't want to invade her privacy; however, many women will be happy to share this with you, plus it can bring you closer together.

Drop those extra pounds – both male and female fertility improves if you're at a healthy weight, so don't think that just because you're male, you're excluded from this. Low sperm count can impact infertility and one reason for this is obesity. With that in mind, it's time to take care of your body too. Exercise and diet both play a role in this, so be sure to take your health seriously. If you have any issues or concerns, visit your doctor, and talk. Sometimes men ignore the signs and symptoms of illness, but your family needs you!

Eat healthily – we have mentioned diet above and this is extremely important. It's important to ensure your body gets the nutrients it needs to keep your sperm count healthy. Some foods can negatively impact your sperm count, including processed meats, soy products, trans fats, dairy products that are high in fat, and, bisphenol A (BPA) and pesticides. Foods that have a positive impact include fruits and vegetables, walnuts, and fish.

Don't…

Smoke – we all know that smoking damages your health, so if you want to conceive, neither of you should smoke. Smoking decreases sperm quality in men and can severely impact sperm health. It can therefore be misshapen, be unable to swim well, and it can also cause DNA damage. Smoking decreases your health and fertility, but second-hand smoke can also decrease the health and fertility of your partner too.

Drink alcohol – while it is important to keep yourself hydrated, alcohol is another factor that can severely impact your sperm count, size, shape, and their ability to swim. Heavy drinking impacts your fertility as it shrinks the testes, changes the way sperm is produced, causes premature or decreased ejaculation, and it lowers your testosterone levels. If you want to conceive, it is best to give up alcohol and concentrate on living a healthy lifestyle which includes taking care of your body through a good diet and exercise.

Use lubrication – lubricants reduce the way that sperm moves, so while they can increase comfort during sex, it harms your sperm. Saliva can also act as a kind of lubricant too. If the sperm is unable to move well, it can't reach the egg in time to fertilize it, therefore conception cannot take place. If you are trying to conceive or are having difficulty conceiving, this is something that both you and your partner should bear in mind.

Helpful Tips for Dads

Sometimes, there are things we wish we had known or been told earlier, when our partners are pregnant, and often our partners wish we had known these things too! Remember, that pregnancy is a learning curve and as every pregnancy is different, nobody is truly an expert. To set your mind at ease, we have provided you with some helpful tips that count in the first month of pregnancy.

1. Remember, your partner isn't sick or made of glass. She won't suddenly break! At this stage, your partner may not know they are carrying a baby, or you may have just found out. You may even be keeping this a secret for now, and while you can change your diet and get excited about becoming parents, it's important to remember that pregnancy is not an illness. She can't break. You don't need to wrap her up in cotton wool, so don't question if everything they do is safe. For instance, if your other half exercised before pregnancy, it's important to remember that most exercise is still safe at this stage. Try to be normal, while also being there to discuss any worries. It's okay to be excited!

2. Replace nights out, with dates – if you go out often, together or with friends, it can be difficult to get into a new routine. Try going out earlier but take your partner out for food or to see a movie (or anything else she enjoys doing). She should avoid alcohol, but you can support her by avoiding it too.

Encourage her to try non-alcoholic beverages and go home early for an early night. You can still catch up with friends but leave earlier than usual.

3. Your partner will be tired, which can also mean mood swings – encourage early nights, nutritious meals, and warm baths. Be sure to chip in with the cleaning, if possible, too. Her body is changing, but most of all, she just needs you to be there. While she doesn't want you to act too different, embrace her often so she feels secure and loved! Brain fog is also real during pregnancy so go easy on her; she'll be frustrated. This is due to hormonal changes.

Reflecting on the First Month

Congratulations on the new pregnancy!

While we've covered a lot in this chapter, hopefully, you've been able to get greater insight into the first month of pregnancy and are getting used to the idea of becoming a parent. Conception is a tricky thing and for some, it takes a little time, so be patient.

If you and your partner are trying for a baby but it hasn't happened yet, it can be frustrating. To finish off this chapter, let's explore 7 top fertility questions:

1. *How can I boost my fertility?* We've discussed how you can boost fertility throughout the first chapter of this book, and this includes living a healthy lifestyle and maintaining a healthy weight. You can also take vitamin supplements, such

as folic acid, zinc, ad coenzyme Q10. If you smoke or drink excessive alcohol, it's a good idea to quit.

2. *We have been trying for a baby for a year, but why have we still not conceived?* It can be easy to feel guilty in this instance, but you shouldn't. Many factors impact fertility. Things like stress, lifestyle, and poor diet or exercise all contribute. If you're concerned, you should visit your doctor. You can go with your partner if you wish.

3. *If I'm infertile, how will I know?* Being infertile is not something you necessarily know, because typically, there are no symptoms. Of course, premature ejaculation and erectile dysfunction can link to infertility, but they are not necessarily signs or symptoms. Conception can take time, but if it takes longer than 12 months, it's a good idea to speak to a fertility doctor or specialist.

4. *Do I have erectile dysfunction?* Erectile dysfunction often occurs due to psychological or physical causes. For example, a person who is obese could be affected, as could a person with depression. When you are fertile, erectile dysfunction can cause anxiety when it comes to your sexual performance. Certain medications, such as testosterone supplements can interfere with sperm production so ensure you talk through your options with your doctor.

5. *I've had a vasectomy. If I have this reversed, will fertility be impacted?* It is possible to have children following a vasectomy reversal, but it isn't guaranteed. Your urologist or

specialist will analyze sperm samples over the next few months, and they will be able to tell you the outcome. They can also help you improve your fertility by making suggestions or offering further treatments.

6. *My partner is receiving fertility treatment, but can I still drink alcohol?* You can, but you should limit this. If you have more than 7 servings, cutting back should help with conception. If possible, it is better to cut this out, but due to the stress fertility causes, some people choose to have an occasional glass of wine. Of course, it is recommended that a person who is pregnant ceases their alcohol consumption once pregnant.

7. *Can we still have sex if we're receiving fertility treatment?* If you're having fertility treatment, protected sex is still generally encouraged. This is because decreases the medical aspect of conception, but it increases intimacy between you and your partner. Other forms of sexual activity, such as touch, oral, or masturbation which encourage pleasure, are not recommended because an orgasm can impact the embryo transfer. You should discuss this with your doctor to ensure you have clarity on this matter.

Now you're at the end of the first month of pregnancy, it's time to move on to the second month. If you're not quite there and conception still awaits, just remember one thing…

Even miracles take a little time."

— CINDERELLA'S FAIRY GODMOTHER

You'll get there soon, and you can 100% be there for your partner because we got your back!

2 THE SECOND MONTH

You've reached month two of pregnancy, congratulations.
She's newly pregnant, so there's so much to learn and so much to do, and it's likely that you're still getting used to the idea of becoming a parent. In this chapter, we'll start to explore what happens in weeks 5-8 so you know what to expect. We'll also talk through some of the things the pregnant person should avoid, as well as some of the things you should do if you want to support your partner well. As we explore the second month of pregnancy, we'll also consider some helpful hints and tips to help you throughout this time. She's likely experiencing some symptoms of pregnancy that are uncomfortable, so it's important to be kind and patient.

Incredible Fact #2

Did you know that babies cry within the womb? A lot of people don't realize this. Although, it is different from how they cry once they're born. It certainly looks different, anyway!

A 2005 study found that a baby in the womb reacts in 5 different ways. They are quite awake, quiet sleep, active awake, active state, or they are crying.

If you were witnessing a baby cry in the womb, you would see that it first inhales, opens its mouth, and takes three quick breaths but the final breath will include a pause as the baby inhales, with a long breath out as they settle again. Your baby won't start crying until around the 20-week mark, so this won't be happening just yet.

Pregnancy Weeks 5-8

Your baby is about the same size as an orange seed at 5 weeks and with the high levels of the pregnancy hormone in your body, a test will certainly show the pregnancy now. As the hormones circulate, they maintain your placenta. Breast growth tissue is also stimulated, and the muscles of your uterus contract.

When women are asked how far along, they are in the pregnancy, they usually answer in weeks here, rather than months. By the end of the second month, your baby will be the size of a raspberry.

The embryo is super small, as it begins to turn into a fetus, but it has a little tail now too. You can head to the doctor now to confirm your pregnancy and they'll help you figure out your due date.

Your baby's heartbeat is visible on ultrasound from weeks 6-7, as it's developing its organs and main bodily systems. Your baby's brain and spinal cord are starting to form too. Towards the end of the month, the baby will be starting to take shape, as it gets its arms and legs.

The mother may be suffering from morning sickness, bloating, and fatigue now, due to the changes the body is dealing with. We'll talk about how you can deal with that, throughout the chapter.

Pregnancy No-Gos

When a person is pregnant, there are many things they should do to ensure that themselves and the baby stay as healthy as possible. There are also many things they should avoid too, which is why we've compiled a list of no-go actions.

Avoid smoking! – smoking (including passive smoking) during pregnancy can severely impact your health and the health of your baby. It can cause an early birth, developmental defects, stillbirth, and it can also hinder growth, which means your baby could be smaller than it should be. Quitting isn't always easy, but it's best for the baby if you and your partner quit as soon as possible.

No drinking alcohol! – your baby is unable to process alcohol as its liver is the last organ to develop and mature, so alcohol should therefore be avoided by expectant mothers when trying to conceive, and throughout the entirety of the pregnancy. When a pregnant person consumes alcohol, it passes through the placenta and increases the risk of miscarriage. It can cause your baby to have a low birth weight and can trigger premature birth. More serious conditions can occur too which will impact your child post-birth such as FASD. FASD (Fetal Alcohol Spectrum Disorder) can result in future speech issues, developmental issues in the joints, bones, and muscles, emotional and social issues, and hyperactivity.

Avoid raw and undercooked meats! – undercooked and raw meat can carry the toxoplasma parasite. While this is generally a mild illness for most people, it can harm a baby and cause serious health issues. It is also linked to miscarriage, stillbirth, or the unexpected loss of a baby at birth. Undercooked meat also carries the risk of salmonella, and while the immune system would usually protect you, it changes when you are carrying a baby, so you are more susceptible. While this may not harm the baby directly, it can make expectant mothers feel extremely ill and weak with a headache and abdominal pains. It can also cause dehydration due to a high temperature, severe vomiting, and diarrhea, so it's best to avoid such meats.

Don't eat deli meat – the Center for Disease Control recommends that pregnant women avoid consuming deli meat, and this is because it can carry listeria bacteria. This causes food poisoning, and although the risk of having this is low, it can be extremely debilitating for a pregnant mother. If they want to eat deli meat, ensure it's extremely fresh and heated up to 165 degrees.

Avoid unpasteurized dairy products – when a dairy product is unpasteurized, it's made with raw milk. Cheeses such as Camembert, Gorgonzola, Brie, and Feta are all types of cheeses to avoid, and the pregnant person should also avoid soft Mexican-style cheese should also be avoided, however, many kinds of cheese are safe.

No hot tubs or saunas – a pregnant person should avoid using anything that will raise their body temperature dramatically, as this can cause defects in the baby's brain or spinal cord. Spending 10 minutes in a hot tub or a sauna can significantly increase your body temperature, so it's higher than 38.3 Celsius. It's certainly something a pregnant lady should avoid.

Limit caffeine intake – if you or your partner are pregnant, caffeine consumption should be limited. Caffeine can impact fetal growth and it can also increase the blood pressure of the expectant mother. It's recommended that they should take no more than 200mg of caffeine per day. That's approximately two small cups of coffee!

Don't clean out the cat litter box – cat feces and its litter often contain toxoplasma, and this can cause increase the risk of miscarriage or stillbirth. We've discussed toxoplasma and its dangers when we discussed raw meats earlier in this section. If you must clean up after the cat, you should use disposable gloves and wash your hands thoroughly.

Avoid certain medications – when you're pregnant, it's important to avoid certain medications as some medication is dangerous for your unborn child and can cause birth defects. For example, over-the-counter medications such as Pepto-Bismol, decongestants such as pseudoephedrine or phenylephrine, some cough and colds medicines, or pain medication such as ibuprofen, aspirin, and naproxen should be avoided. Some acne medications, seizure medication, blood thinners, and various depression, anxiety, blood pressure, and arthritis medication can also cause birth defects. The best thing to do is read the instructions and if you're not certain it's safe, seek advice from a medical or healthcare professional.

Don't use oil-based paints when painting – while there aren't many studies that look at the impact of painting on pregnancy, there are chemicals that a pregnant person should avoid. Oil-based paints contain harsh solvents so the fumes they release can cause eye irritation, nausea, headaches, fatigue, and dizziness. Regular exposure to solvents is known to impact the baby's head size and cause growth restrictions in babies, like those with fetal alcohol syndrome.

Month Two To-Do List

While it's only month 2, your newly pregnant partner is most likely experiencing a few uncomfortable symptoms. There's so much to do between now and the birth of your child, but at this stage, it's important to be as kind and patient as possible.

You probably feel like you don't know what to do exactly, and that's a normal feeling to have. Nobody tells us what we should or should not be doing at this point, but there are so many ways you can support your pregnant partner:

- Cook more – your partner would love nothing more than to have some of their meals cooked for them in the early days. She'll likely be extra tired, feeling sick, and suffering from food aversions. There's no reason why you can't step up, be a grown-up, and cook for yourself (and her) when she's not up to the task. Knock up a healthy vegetable soup, or chicken breast with vegetables – it doesn't have to be complicated, but the more nutritious it is, the better it is for mom and baby.

- See food as fuel – right now, her energy is low, so she needs some natural energy boosts. You can help with this by ensuring she's drinking enough water – when you grab a drink for yourself, get her one too. Oatmeal is a great source of vitamin B, iron, and zinc, which means it's great at boosting energy, so knock up a bowl for your partner for breakfast. Other foods such as nuts, spinach, apple, mangoes, and sweet potatoes are also good energy sources, so when you make her something to eat, try to incorporate foods that will kickstart her energy levels.

- Handle the moodiness – your partner's hormones will be going crazy, and you must handle their mood swings without reacting in anger. Showing anger causes stress and anxiety, so it can cause distress for the baby. Just remember, this isn't personal! When dealing with moodiness, try to stay calm and allow the emotional time to de-escalate. It's okay to be assertive when expressing yourself, as long as you remain respectful and while you may take some of the responsibility, you may require your partner to do the same. Leading the way can encourage this. Make sure you're patient and compassionate when communicating with your other-half and validate how they feel and try to understand it. Wait until your partner is calm before you address any challenges and remember to reflect on your actions. Pick your battles – sometimes we just have to agree to disagree, so don't drag out pointless disagreements, and don't try to control or change your partner. Just work to be a positive influence and alleviate any issues by listening and being supportive, but honest too. Your partner will appreciate it!

- Your pregnant partner may be suffering from fatigue, morning sickness, tender breasts, bloating, and moodiness, but there are some ways that you can help to ease some of her symptoms:

o Fatigue – if your partner is suffering from fatigue, there are some things you can do to help, for instance, ensure she stays hydrated, eats regularly, and even run a warm bath to help her relax and wind down. Encouraging light exercise can be good too, even if it's just a walk as it can help her sleep through the night. There's also no reason why she shouldn't have a short nap throughout the day, especially if she's having difficulty sleeping at night.

o Morning sickness – this is a common sign of pregnancy in the early stages, usually throughout months 2-3. Despite the name associating it with 'morning' time, it can happen any time during the day or night. Keeping up with regular snacks or sipping ginger ale can sometimes help to relieve the sickly feeling. It's possible to buy medication over the counter too. If the morning sickness is severe, it can cause dehydration, and you may need to take your partner to see a medical professional.

o Breast pain – if your partner is suffering from breast pain during the early stages of pregnancy, it can feel uncomfortable. This is often the first sign of pregnancy reported by women, but their body is starting to make changes so that they can grow their little human and keep it safe and healthy. The hormones in your body are getting your breasts ready for breastfeeding, so the milk ducts are growing. To remedy breast pain, your partner should wear super supportive bras. They could also increase their water intake, eat flaxseeds, and use warm compresses on the breast area.

o Bloating – if your partner feels bloated, they'll feel uncomfortable, but bloating is a common early sign of pregnancy. To avoid bloating, your partner could ensure they are eating a well-balanced diet, which is full of whole grains, vegetables, and beans as all these foods are rich in fiber, which can alleviate bloating symptoms. It's a good idea to eat smaller meals, but more frequently, avoid caffeine, and drink at least 8 glasses of water each day. They should avoid foods that cause gas, such s broccoli, cauliflower, sprouts, and cabbage, as well as high-fat foods and alcohol. All these things cause bloating!

o Mood swings – mood swings occur in pregnancy due to stress, tiredness, and changes to your hormones and metabolism. Hormones impact the way your body communicates with your brain and impact how your body releases your brain chemicals that regulate your mood. Mood swings are very common between the 6th and 10th week of pregnancy. While there is no direct cure, you should encourage your partner to rest, take a nap, eat well, exercise well, and take relaxing breaks throughout the day. Simply spending time with your partner can help with their mood, so watch a video, go for a walk, and encourage them not to be hard on themselves. You can even book them in for a massage too or encourage them to go to a yoga or meditation class aimed at pregnant women. Sometimes just being there and showing your support, both emotionally and physically, can make a difference.

o   Clean the litter box – if you or your partner have a cat, be sure to change the litter box. We've already talked about cat feces and litter trays, and how they can impact pregnant women, so take that worry away – do it for her!

o   Step up around the house – you can support your partner by stepping up around the house. If your partner is suffering from any of the early pregnancy symptoms we've mentioned in this chapter, she'll appreciate you doing the heavy lifting, getting out the vacuum, and helping out with the cooking. In fact, why not make up extra batches of food, so she can grab something quick on the days she's extra tired? While pitching in his great, don't forget to listen to your partner too, and encourage her to rest and relax. Help her make the right choices when it comes to alcohol and smoking and encourage a healthier lifestyle that incorporates exercise and healthy eating. Get involved in the process by staying informed, as this will also help you prepare.

o   Is she taking her vitamin supplements? – it's important that your partner is taking folic acid supplements for the first 3 months of pregnancy, as this improves brain and spinal cord development in the early stages of pregnancy. Your partner should also be keeping up with their iron as this ensures you have a steady flow of oxygen in your blood to the fetus. Iron supports the development of the fetus and placenta, and other vitamins such as calcium and vitamin help the development of your baby's bones and teeth. Prenatal vitamin supplements help the development of your baby while helping the expectant mother stay fit and well too.

The Trials of Being a Modern Dad

Being a modern dad isn't easy because a lot is resting on our shoulders. When I was young, my father worked long hours because he felt it was his responsibility to provide for his family. Due to his hard work, my mother stayed at home and took care of the kids and the house. There were no childcare options like there are today, so in many households, mom took care of the kids and the home. However, dad was seen as the authority figure, so nobody wanted mom to tell dad if we'd misbehaved. Due to his long working hours and busy work life, dad rarely got involved in parenting, other than disciplining anyway. He kept a roof over our heads, he kept us fed and clothed, and yes, thanks to him, we had a good life.

I'm not saying this wrong – this was just the way things were done, but times have changed. I love my dad. I'm lucky enough to have a close family and things changed over time, but most of my childhood memories are with my mom and siblings. I didn't want that for my children, as I want them to have fun and happy memories with me too.

Today, things are different, and many fathers play a more active role in the lives of their children, but this presents many challenges. Many dads are hands-on, they cook, clean, and change diapers, which are tasks that fathers just didn't do generations ago. While many dads still feel a strong sense of responsibility to provide for their family, more and more also spread themselves thin because they want to spend time with their kids, they want to parent them and make memories, and they want to build strong bonds. But this isn't always easy.

Men are not always known for publicly embracing others, showing emotion, or opening up when they find things tough or stressful. When you add being a new dad to that equation, you are at risk of taking on too much and this takes its toll.

If you're going to be there for your partner through this pregnancy, you need to take care of yourself too. If you're feeling the pressure of being the 'rock' for your family (like most dads do), and begin to feel stressed or depressed, you owe it to yourself and your family to do something about this. Three out of four dads feel increased levels of stress when they try to manage their work-life balance.

Did you know that depression is common in men, and studies show that 26% of men show signs of depression within 3-6 months after their babies are born? The health of a new dad is something that is largely overlooked, but that's because so many men suffer alone, rather than seeking help. It took me a while to realize, but it's okay, not to be okay.

More and more pressure is placed on fatherhood, and while it's tough at times, it can be the best experience of your life. Nobody teaches us how to be a good dad or partner, but it is figure-out-able. Keeping a stiff upper lip and suffering in silence is no longer the cool thing to do, so as a modern dad, it's time to lead the way by speaking out, embracing fatherhood, and painting a true picture of it, while acknowledging every bump along the way.

Be honest with her about how you feel, ask her advice, and talk about the real things that lie ahead for you both. She'll appreciate your honesty, so don't let your well-being suffer as it will not only affect you but your family, in the long term.

There are so many benefits to your child and the whole family when dad plays a more active role. Studies have shown that kids do better in school, have better health, and even get higher grades when both parents play an active role in their lives. So, make the most of your bonding time, from the time of birth (or before… we'll let you know when your little one can hear you). All you got to do as a dad, is lead by example, keep learning, and provide love, support, and honesty to your family. While times change, dads still have an important part to play in their child's life. It's time to live like the new generation of modern fathers and be the best we can be.

 My father didn't tell me how to live; he lived and let me watch him do it."

— CLARENCE BUDINGTON KELLAND, AUTHOR.

Helpful Tips for Dad

It's no secret that dads-to-be often say inappropriate things when supporting their partners. It's like we have no control over it; it just happens. Your partner is extra sensitive when pregnant, especially at first, because her hormones are whizzing around like a school of frenzied piranhas, searching for prey. Don't be the prey – don't say the wrong thing…

I'm going to let you know three things that most men believe are myths. Believing they are myths can get you in all kinds of trouble. You only know, what you know, so take note of the myths below:

1. Pregnancy brain is NOT a myth – the neurotransmitters in your partner's brain will not be getting the messages from the brain if the hormones are not functioning effectively. She will forget where her keys are, but she'll feel like she's losing her mind. Don't fuel the fire and make pregnancy-brain jokes unless she initiates them first.

2. If she says 'it's fine that you have four pillows' when she has two, it's not fine – she needs more pillows than you do right now. Her body is changing, so offer her extra pillows. A pillow between the knees or behind her back or supporting her bump may just be the key to her getting a couple of extra hours of sleep. If she sleeps better, she feels better, and her mood improves.

3. There's a difference between tiredness and laziness – while most men love to joke, it's guaranteed that making jokes about your partner being lazy when they're exhausted will not work in your favor, in fact, heads will likely roll. Her

body is preparing itself for a long pregnancy followed by the birth of a baby, and it takes a lot out of a person. Every meal she has will give the best bits to the baby, so her needs are already coming in second. If your body started to expand and someone was removing the best parts of your food before it got to you, it's likely you wouldn't look or feel so hot either. Support her, by stepping up.

Second Month Q & A

It's common for you and your partner to have many questions at this stage, so we've selected four of the most common questions during the second month. Let's discuss:

1. *My partner is pregnant but is bleeding. What should we do?*

It's always best to seek medical attention as soon as possible, in this instance. Some people do have bleeding or spotting in early pregnancy, but if you or your partner do bleed or spot, you should contact your midwife or doctor for advice. In some cases, this is normal, as women release 2 eggs from the ovaries every month, so light bleeding or spotting can be linked to the breakdown of the other egg, however, bleeding is also a sign of miscarriage.

2. *When do pregnancy cravings begin?*

This is a tough question, because some people report cravings in the very early stages of pregnancy, such as at 5 weeks, while others get no cravings throughout the whole pregnancy. Cravings are different for everyone, and some are even strange. One person may crave specific meals, while others may want fatty or sweet foods, and then another may want unusual combinations of food, such as pickles with ice cream, or chocolate with bacon. If your partner starts craving coal, soil, toothpaste, or other non-food items, it's worth speaking to a healthcare professional as this can be a sign that they have a vitamin deficiency.

3. My partner and I aren't ready to tell everyone we're having a baby yet, as it's still in the early stages. She's exhausted at work, but what should she do?

Your partner would be best speaking directly to her line manager and explaining her situation and that she doesn't want anyone else to know as even family are not aware yet. That way, the manager may be more sympathetic and could help her come up with a solution, such as working more flexibly or allowing in some extra breaks, or time off if need be. While it's not ideal, sometimes it's necessary and she may find that the business has procedures in place to support her.

4. Is the flu vaccine safe?

Yes. The flu jab will help you protect yourself and your baby against the flu, regardless of what stage you are in pregnancy. Being pregnant impacts your natural immune system, which is why the flu vaccine is recommended in the first place. Catching the flu during pregnancy can cause complications for the mother and child.

You're at the end of your second month of pregnancy, so you're already a fifth of the way into your pregnancy. This means we'll be looking at the third month in chapter 3, which is the final part of the first pregnancy trimester. Get ready to discover how your family dynamics will change, while exploring the development of your baby during the 9–13-week stage.

Prepare to be amazed!

THE THIRD MONTH

This month marks the end of the first trimester of pregnancy, which means things are getting real now. It's normal to start to prepare for the future at this point of the pregnancy, so this chapter will reflect on the development of your baby at 9-13 weeks, as well as exploring how the family dynamics will change once your little one arrives.

We'll also explore the things you can do as a supportive partner and dad-to-be, as there is so much to do. We're not going to leave it there, as we've also put together some ways to support your partner in the ways they need at this stage of pregnancy.

The truth is, you've made it to the end of the first trimester and this is a huge pregnancy milestone. It's mostly uphill from here – well that's the case at least for dads…

Most people choose to keep the pregnancy quiet until the first ultrasound appointment at approximately 12 weeks has taken place. But nobody is the same. When it comes to pregnancy, we sometimes need people to confide in, especially if we have any worries or concerns. It's a good idea to talk to your partner about how they're feeling, and how you're feeling, and decide when the best time is to tell others that you're going to be parents. While sometimes we say we'll keep it quiet until the end of the first trimester, sometimes it simply comes out.

When a work colleague of mine found out his wife was pregnant with their first baby, they didn't tell anyone until the end of the first trimester. He was a party animal and was well-known for his immature actions if he consumed too much alcohol. He was the person who always had too much to drink, knocked drinks over on the table, insulted the big guys playing pool, so the rest of us had to stop the fight, or said something inappropriate to a woman in a bar. He would come into work sometimes hungover, to the point he'd find somewhere quiet to take a nap so when he got married, we made fun of the day he would become a dad and believed it would be far in the future (if it ever arrived at all). Don't get me wrong, he was a good worker, but he was irresponsible and immature in life. We couldn't imagine him being a father, because, in our eyes, he could barely care for himself, and we were forever digging him out of trouble.

We didn't know his wife was pregnant at the time, but we were still making jokes about pregnancy changing his life. We left diapers, baby food, and pacifiers on his desk, and told jokes or horror stories about parenting. His behavior started to change and for a few weeks, he didn't seem like his 'usual' self. It wasn't until we went for a few drinks (which turned into too many for him) that he told us all his wife was 10 weeks pregnant. He and his wife had agreed to tell nobody until after the first ultrasound, but he couldn't help it – he was spooked! It turned out he was really scared about becoming a dad and our so-called banter wasn't helping. It was the first time we'd ever seen him emotional, but that night, the fun-loving party animal, sobered up, had his first adult conversation with the boys at a respectable diner, and returned home coherent at a reasonable hour.

We were all sworn to secrecy about the pregnancy but I'm sure Becky, his wife, was suspicious – it was the first time he'd ever gone home before midnight while still having full use of his legs. *Who wouldn't be suspicious?*

While my colleague didn't mean for this to come out, he did have genuine concerns that he was bottling up inside. The best thing you can do is talk to your partner as the best outcome is to tell everyone together, at a time you both agree upon. If you bottle up how you feel, you could end up blurting it out too. Acceptance is key here, as we all must accept that sometimes things don't go to plan. Accept that both you and your partner are capable of making mistakes and that it's completely normal to have a wobble, especially if you're becoming a parent for the first time.

Now, let's look at our crazy baby fact for month 3 – it's a 'tall' order.

Incredible Fact #3

This is going to sound out there, but an obstetrician's study confirms that tall women are more likely to have twins. Obstetrician, Gary Steinman believes that this is due to a growth factor, which is similar to insulin, is links both height and twining. His study found that those who gave birth to multiple children were more than an inch taller than the average American-born woman. He says that the growth factor can stimulate the follicle of the hormone which then modifies the sensitivity of the ovary.

Pregnancy Weeks 9-13

During weeks 9-13, your baby will grow well, and the expectant mother will experience a lot of changes and side effects. At 9 weeks, the baby is starting to look more human. Their arms and legs are forming and moving well, which means the muscles are starting to develop. They have all the essential body parts including elbows, knees, nose, upper lip, eyelids, and toes. Their tooth buds are also starting to develop within the gum, although it will take another week or so before the teeth begin to harden within the jaw.

The placenta is taking care of your baby and it ensures it has everything it needs. The placenta is now in control of producing hormones to help your baby grow and is connected to it through the umbilical cord. While it's too early to feel movement yet, they are beginning to develop their hearing. Their heart is also big enough to hear too, through a handheld ultrasound device, although, as your baby is small and moves a lot, it's not always possible to locate the sound easily. While it will start this month at the size of a green olive, by the 13th week, it will be approximately the size of a lemon.

When you get to the tenth week of pregnancy, your baby is no longer referred to as an embryo, but a fetus. Bones and cartilage are forming within its body and it's getting stronger every day. Teeth are also starting to harden within the gums. The main parts of the eyes are also fully formed. By week 11, your baby will have bulges within its developing brain, but they are only temporary. Their spinal cord development is the key to baby being able to move their limbs effectively.

During week 12 of pregnancy, the baby's intestines that have been taking up the umbilical cord space are now moving back into the stomach area. Their body is starting to produce white blood cells now, created by their bone marrow. Their digestive system is also starting to work, and the expectant mother is likely to have an antinatal appointment or check-up, which will allow you to hear your baby's heartbeat. Typically, your baby's first ultrasound will take place at around 12 weeks, but sometimes it's slightly earlier or later. The ultrasound allows you to date your pregnancy more closely.

By the time your baby reaches 13 weeks, their vocal cords will start to form and their eyes will continue to develop, however, their eyelids will remain closed for some time. Prior to this, your baby's head will seem large in proportion to its body, but it will start to be in proportion from this stage. The expectant mother is one-third of the way through the pregnancy, which means, the first trimester reaches an end.

Changing Dynamics

There's no doubt that your life as you know it is about to change, and this means that you'll have to adapt. While many people stress over this, it's because they don't know what to expect. When you know what to expect, it doesn't take long to realize that change can be a positive thing.

When you're a first-time parent, a baby means a big change for you both. While going out for a bite to eat, a movie, or sleeping in, won't be as simple as it once was, it is not impossible although you will have more things to consider, like sitters and feeding the baby. Some new parents don't even feel like going anywhere at all following the birth of their baby, and that's okay too. Often this is due to lack of sleep, as even if your baby is good at sleeping, you still won't be getting the high-quality sleep you once were.

If you already have other children, you'll have even more changes to contend with which will require more planning. You'll need to introduce the baby into family life while ensuring you're still providing care and time to your others – this can require adjusting your expectations.

The key to dealing with the changing dynamics is to not expect too much of yourself or your partner – take everything in your stride and be patient. It's easy to worry about what will happen to 'us' time when you're new parents but it's all about preparation and working together. Your newborn will sleep regularly, so if you both complete the tasks and chores you need to do, you'll be able to snatch moments together, in fact, you may have time to watch a movie. Some people have sitters on hand (often in the form of family members or close friends), but as everyone's situation is different and therefore, it's impossible to refer to individual circumstances. Think about some other ways you could spend time together, by even one of you cooking dinner for the other one, or maybe, with some careful planning, you could still eat out by taking the baby with you. If you're baby forms a routine quite quickly, you may even time this when it's baby's nap time. If you don't master it straight away, don't worry, it's a process.

As you adjust to your role as mom or dad, the experience will make you more confident, especially as you get to know your little one. If you have other children in the house, it's important to remember that they all have different reactions to siblings. You should get your children used to the idea of being a big brother or sister, to help them adjust to their role. They may resist or need some time, but they need love and patience from you, so they can start to accept their new sibling. Introduce the baby slowly, and in a calm way, with your re-assurance.

Make sure you each spend time with your other children too, as they need to feel equally important. You should make them aware of their role as a big sister or brother, and provide reassurance that mom and dad love them, but also love baby. Your child will often adjust and mirror your behavior, but if there are some behavior issues, your child will need your support and attention.

Alone time is more important than ever. You could take out your child to do something they enjoy or play a game, then you could spend time with your newborn while your other half has time alone with the older child. If their acting out but are too young to com-municate it, explain in language they understand and try to understand the root of the matter. Communication is really im-portant!

Even if there's only you and your partner, with your newborn, com-munication is key. Talk through how you can strengthen your relationship before your baby makes an appearance and discuss how you can support each other. For example, if your partner is tired, consider how you can help and listen to each other. This is some-thing you may have to practice, but there are two key questions you can ask each other:

- How are you feeling?
- What can I do to assist?

If you have other children, it's a good idea to model listening and mutual respect to your child, as well as love and affection for one another. It can even encourage your child to ask questions or express any concerns they have.

Month Three To-Do List

Your other half may still be suffering from a lot of the symptoms mentioned in month 2, so you can still support her with those (as discussed in chapter 2). In addition to this, there may be additional symptoms to consider too.

Her waistline is expanding, and she may notice that her clothes are becoming tight around her abdomen. Reassure her she is beautiful, as this may make her feel self-conscious or nervous.

Make sure she's taking her prenatal vitamins – this is extremely important as baby is going through a key development stage as it transforms from an embryo to a fetus. Lack of certain vitamins can result in developmental issues, so they'll help to keep the baby healthy.

Healthy eating will help her maintain her energy, even though she's tired right now, so ensure she's eating well.

Capture memories and make the pregnancy exciting by documenting it with regular pictures. Take pictures when you're doing things together, or when you're buying or doing something baby-related.

Some people also take a side-view picture of the pregnant person every week, to document the growth of her pregnancy belly.

By the time you reach the end of the month, it's generally time to start telling people that your partner is pregnant. Of course, there isn't a set time, so some people prefer to keep it quiet for a while longer while others tell people earlier. You may wish to investigate maternity and paternity leave policies at work.

Maternity leave differs across the world, and between businesses. In the US, maternity leave is around 12 weeks, but many women find that they are not eligible for this. Your partner needs to find out what leave they are entitled to by looking at their workplace policies. This way, they can work out how long they can be off work once they have their baby and it helps you work out your financials too. Your leave could be paid or unpaid, and this could impact how much time you feel able to take off.

When it comes to paternity leave, the US does not have a law that ensures fathers get paid leave following the birth of a child, however, some businesses do offer paid or unpaid time off work. Again, contact your workplace to find out what is available to you. Paternity leave is common in other countries, but not so much in the US, but it's certainly something to consider as bonding in the early days has proven benefits.

Having a baby is a life-changing moment, and many parents decide that one of them will be a stay-at-home parent. You should discuss this openly with your partner and review your financials. Sometimes, this isn't possible, some parents decide to work around each other, to save on childcare costs, while others start their own business. You both have time to think about your options. If you start planning now and working out how you'll deal with any shortfall, it will alleviate the stress as it prevents you from having to resolve this later down the line. It's also important to look at your healthcare coverage, so you can see what costs you and your partner are responsible for during the pregnancy and beyond.

If you're concerned about anything pregnancy related, don't be afraid to reach out to other dads for advice. You're not alone in this, and experienced dads may know something you don't, so just ask. *What do you have to lose?*

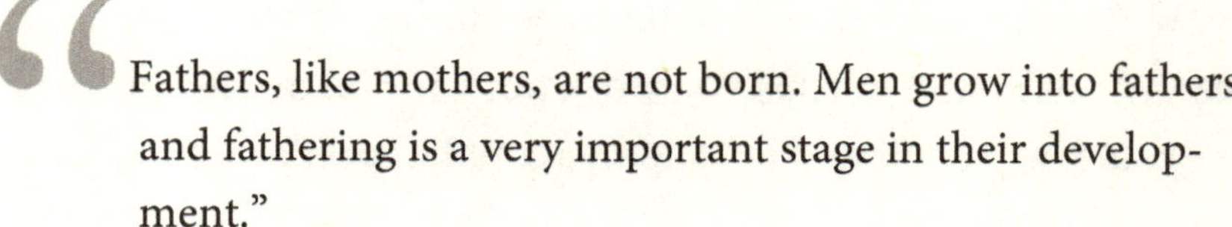

Fathers, like mothers, are not born. Men grow into fathers and fathering is a very important stage in their development."

— DAVID GOTTESMAN

How to Survive Month 3 and Stay in Her Good Books

Now, from time to time we do get things wrong. We may have good intentions, but it can be difficult for us to know what our partner wants or needs throughout their pregnancy. The third month can be a frustrating time as she's starting to put on weight, her clothes are uncomfortable, and she's extremely tired and hormonal. One wrong move and you could be in trouble!

If you want to stay in her good books, there are some things you need to know…

1. She doesn't want you to label her as hormonal – yes, she is hormonal, but she knows it, she doesn't need you to remind her. Even if she's crying because the jumpsuit you bought was the wrong shade of white, or if she's angry because you cooked chicken instead of steak for dinner, try and move past it without mentioning the 'H' word. Simply comfort her and try to remedy the situation.

2. She's worried she won't be a good mom – just like you're worried you won't be a good dad. This is all new, and if she's already battling the exhaustion, she probably doesn't know how on earth she's going to deal with a baby and its overnight feed.

3. She's excited to see you rise to the occasion when it comes to fatherhood – she already knows you're going to make a good dad, and that's why she's with you. She can't wait to see the baby in your arms, while your face beams with pride. Showing you're going to be a great dad by stepping up and supporting her now only makes the excitement greater. Share in her excitement and even build on that with her by expressing how excited you are. It will certainly lift her spirits and remind her that it's all worthwhile.

4. She appreciates you – she might not always tell you, but she does. You're her rock and her superhero. Keep stepping up and involving yourself in the pregnancy. She needs you!

Third Month Q & A

It's the end of the first trimester, and you'll certainly have lots of questions. We're addressing three common questions below:

1. When should the expectant mother arrange to see a midwife?

It's best to make an appointment with a midwife as soon as you find out you're expecting. Your midwife will provide you with lots of useful information and will help you plan, to ensure you get the best care for you and your baby.

2. How can my pregnant partner get a midwife?

A midwife will be assigned to you, or you'll be referred to them, via your doctor or your doctor's practice. Usually, you just call and speak to the receptionist, and they'll book your first appointment.

3. When does the mother start to feel the baby kick or move?

As you head into the second trimester, you won't have long to wait. This does vary, but some moms can feel kicking as early as 14 weeks, while others don't feel anything until they are approximately 26 weeks. If there's any concern, you should speak to your midwife or another medical professional.

Congratulations! You're heading into the second trimester of pregnancy. There's so much to look forward to as you head into the next chapter. We're going to talk over weeks 14-17, and you won't be disappointed.

THE FOURTH MONTH

The pregnancy is now in its second trimester, which means you and your other half have probably had your first ultrasound and have started telling people that you're expecting. Your other half is probably starting to feel well now as the signs of early pregnancy wear off, and you're both settled or settling into the idea that you're going to have a little one in less than half of a year, *but what's next?*

Don't worry, there's still plenty going on. In this chapter, we'll focus on the development of your child during weeks 14-17, and we'll also take a slightly different angle here as we discuss pregnancy and exercise throughout this trimester, exploring its benefits, as well as what she should or shouldn't do during this stage.

This point is generally the sweet spot of pregnancy, as the early pregnancy symptoms are passing, but the symptoms of later pregnancy when her bump has grown are not upon her yet – they generally start in the third trimester.

Incredible Fact #4

Women's feet can grow by a whole shoe size during pregnancy! This is only temporary though as your feet are not actually growing. The ligaments that hold your bones together are more relaxed, which allows your feet to spread. This happens because the hormone, relaxin, is produced as this helps to prepare your body by loosening the ligaments in your pelvis.

It then reaches your feet, so if your feet appear wider or longer, it's due to this change in the body.

Let's talk about your baby's development – it's exciting stuff!

Pregnancy Weeks 14-17

By week 14, your baby is approximately the size of a kiwi fruit and is kicking and moving well. The head is developing well and it's becoming more rounded as well as being in more proportion. If you have an antenatal appointment or check-up, you'll likely get to listen to your baby's heartbeat through a handheld monitor. Your baby's kidneys are working too, which means they can wee.

Your baby will be making faces, as it can now use its facial muscles, which means it can frown and squint. They will start to grow hair soon as little hair follicles have started to form deep into their skin, which includes their chin, eyebrows, and their upper lip.

All bodily features are moving into the right places, such as the eyes and ears, and while their skin is thin, so their blood vessels, which are still developing, show right through. If an X-ray was performed on your baby, his skeleton would be visible as the bones start to grow and get stronger. Your baby is also at work, as it's practicing its breathing, swallowing, and sucking motions ready for when they're born. By the time your baby is 16 weeks, it will be 4-5 inches (or 10-

13 centimeters) in length and can weigh up to 4 ounces. At this stage, your baby will start to hear you, so if you talk, they can hear your voice. Although, their hearing isn't fully formed for another 2 weeks. They are growing, rapidly, and their eyes are sensitive to light, even though they remain closed.

By 17 weeks, your baby is becoming a master at sucking and swallowing, as they prepare for feeding when they are born. Even their little fingerprints are forming. It's hard to believe that by 17 weeks, everyone is already unique. Your baby's heart is regulated by the brain now and beats twice as fast as your own. At almost 13cm long, they are now the size of a large onion.

It's crazy, that with just 23 weeks left to go, your baby is almost half-way to being born!

Pregnancy and Exercise

Your partner should certainly exercise throughout their pregnancy, as this can help them stay fit and healthy. It can also relieve stress, help to prevent gestational diabetes, and improve your stamina (which is useful when it comes to the delivery of the baby). It can also be beneficial because it improves their posture, and decreases backache, fatigue, and other discomforts.

If you exercise regularly before your pregnancy, you should be able to do this throughout your pregnancy, but remember, this should be in moderation, and you should never exercise at the higher level that you used to. She must do what's comfortable for her and avoid anything that's high-intensity. Low-impact aerobics would be ideal!

It's perfectly safe to exercise throughout pregnancy, but of course, the expectant mother needs to be sensible. For example, they shouldn't suddenly learn to parachute out of an airplane, bungee jump, horse jump, or mountain bike. It is good for her and the baby, but it's important to carefully select the exercises to be on the safe side. Beyond popular belief, exercise proves effective when it comes to pregnancy aches and pains, and it can certainly improve swollen ankles, constipation, bloating, and backache, as well as helping her to sleep. If she sleeps well and feels better, it's better for her, the baby, and you.

Your baby will benefit from having a fitter heart and it will boost their brain health. Their BMI could even be lower as a result. In return she will feel her pregnancy symptoms decrease, a boost in her mood, and postpartum recovery will be faster.

Expectant mums are recommended to exercise for at least 30 minutes every day. The way this is completed is entirely up to the individual. Some women choose to do vigorous chores such as vacuuming, while others prefer to walk for 10 minutes, three times each day. It is a good idea to speak to a practitioner before starting a new exercise program whilst pregnant.

The best types of workouts to complete during pregnancy include swimming, running, walking, aerobics or dance classes, and hiking. Some gym machines, such as a treadmill, can be useful too. Yoga, Tai Chi, and Pilates can be great too.

There are certain exercises that your pregnant partner should avoid as they can be harmful. They include activities such as contact sports (basketball, volleyball, soccer, football), exercises that include holding your breath, exercises that involved extensive jumping (skipping, hopping, bouncing), and exercises that could cause any kind of abdominal trauma, regardless of how mild, waist-twisting exercises, bending deep into the knee, full sit-ups, toe touches while your legs are straight, and double leg raises. You should also avoid long periods of inactivity, then suddenly taking part in heavy spurts of exercise, and in addition, avoid exercising when it's too hot or humid. All these things can be harmful when performed through pregnancy, either to the expectant mom or baby.

Some simple stretches, ideal for the expectant mom, include:

- Neck rotations – make sure you relax the shoulders and neck, drop the head forward, and rotate your head to the left shoulder. Move your head back to the middle, and then repeat on the left. Repeat this four times.

- Shoulder rotations – bring your shoulders forward then circle them by lifting them to the ears, and back down. Repeat this four times.

- Leg shakes – sit down and extend your legs and feet in front of you. Move the legs up and down, alternating them, in a gentle shaking motion. Do this

- Ankle circles – sit down and stretch out your legs and feet in front of you. Ensure your toes are relaxed and rotate your feet. Make sure you use the whole foot and ankle and make large circles.

Kegel (or pelvic floor) exercises are beneficial too, as they help the muscles strengthen in the bladder, bowels, and uterus. To do these, you should imagine that you're trying to stop urinating or passing gas, and you contract those muscles, holding them for 5 seconds before you relax. You mustn't move your butt, abdominal muscles, or your legs whilst doing this. You should do this 10 times each day.

Tailor exercises are often used to relieve low back pain, so they are recommended too. They help to strengthen your hip, thigh, and pelvic muscles too. To complete these exercises, you should sit on the floor:

1. Tailor sit – bend your knees and cross your ankles. You should lean forward slightly, keeping your back straight. Don't tense though, just relax. Hold this position whenever you can, as it will ease any pain in your back.

2. Tailor press – bend your knees and press the bottoms of your feet together. Hold onto your ankles and pull your feet in, towards your body. Put the palms of your hands on your knees and inhale. As you do this, press your knees down against your hands (your hands should be pressing up towards your knees, creating counterpressure). Hold for 5 seconds, then relax.

There are ways to work out safely, so you should encourage your partner to start slowly by only exercising for around 20 minutes. If they are already a regular at the gym, make sure they don't go overboard. They must warm up and cool down well, but make sure you're able to stay cool too. Encourage them to listen to their body, so if something is wrong or they feel in pain, they can respond to this

– for example, if they experience any pain or swelling, they can stop and contact their medical practitioner.

We have already talked about the types of exercises to avoid, but they should also keep off their back, drink plenty of water, and take something to snack on. For pregnant women, it's important to wear breathable, loose, and stretchy clothes, and she'll probably need a support bra too as well as good sneakers that support her feet well. This can reduce the chances of you falling or injuring yourself.

Just remember that her ever-changing pregnancy is putting extra demands on her body, so they need to be considered as she progresses in her pregnancy, and her exercise regime may need to be adjusted. For example, as the baby grows, she may need more oxygen and energy to allow her to give the baby what they need. The changes in hormones can mean she is at greater risk of injury, due to her stretched ligaments, and carrying so much extra weight can shift the center of gravity, putting more stress on her back and pelvic area.

Expectant mothers must stop exercising at once if they experience:

- Pain in their pelvis, abdomen, or persistent contractions
- A headache
- Vaginal bleeding
- A decrease or absence in the movement of the baby
- Dizzy spells, feeling faint, dizzy, light-headed, or nauseated
- Feelings of cold or clamminess
- A trickle of fluid leaks consistently from her vagina, or if she has a sudden gush of fluid
- Shortness of breath

- Difficulty walking
- An irregular heartbeat or if it becomes rapid
- Swelling in her hands, face, or ankles, or suffers from calf pain
- Muscle weakness

In any of the instances above, she should speak to a medical practitioner immediately.

Month Four To-Do List

You're at month four and there's still plenty to do, but we'll make this quick…

- Check in with her – she's probably feeling relief from the earlier pregnancy symptoms, but you should still ask her if she's okay, just to make sure
- Enjoy your time together – she's feeling great so make the most of it
- Keep reminding her to take her prenatal vitamins – they're so important While she might feel great right now, we want her to keep feeling that way
- It's possible that mom's feeling congested, so if he is, you can get nasal strips or sprays that are suitable during pregnancy. A dehumidifier could also help
- She could be suffering from pain in the lower back, so ask her how you can help. Sometimes a massage, some extra pillows or cushions, or a hot-water bottle can help – make sure it's not burning hot though

- Be patient with her, pregnancy brain is real – she may be forgetful due to lack of sleep or stress, but that's okay. It's not entirely sure if pregnancy itself impacts mental sharpness and your memory, but most moms-to-be feel like this. She could use lists and reminders on her smartphone to stay on track with everything

- Mama has cravings! – her cravings can start in the first trimester but can continue throughout the pregnancy. While sometimes she can go off food and feel sickly other times, she'll crave specific foods. The most important thing is to ensure she's eating safely and healthily. Some foods or drinks, like caffeinated or sugary drinks, are not good for her. The foods most commonly craved are fruits, fruit juices, dairy, chocolate, sweets, starchy carbohydrates, pickles and ice cream, and fast foods. Some women even crave spicy or salty foods, while others can crave inedible things, like soil. Cravings are a strange thing that we don't entirely understand, so encourage her to act on her 'good' cravings, but distract her from the bad

- Time to schedule your 20-week ultrasound – this is a full scan of your baby, including its brain, spine, abdomen, limbs, face, and the whole of the heart. It allows everything to be measured and ensures your baby is growing at the right pace. You can also find out the sex of your baby if you wish, but you should discuss this carefully with your partner first, to ensure you're both on the same pace – *do you both want to know, or do you want a surprise?*

Mama Deserves a Massage

Pregnancy takes its toll. While it's a beautiful thing, there are so many symptoms which include aches and pains as your body grows, bears extra weight, and stretches. She deserves a prenatal massage!

Many people believe that massage isn't safe throughout pregnancy, but the truth is, it is after the first trimester. It's important to let the therapist know about the pregnancy, as there are certain oils or pressure points that should be avoided during pregnancy. A pregnant person shouldn't have one during the first trimester. If they do decide to have a massage in the second or third trimester, it's a good idea to get the go-ahead from your medical practitioner too.

A prenatal massage is when adaptations are made to accommodate a person's shape and situation. It may not be possible for the pregnant person to lay on their back as this can disrupt blood flow, as well as putting pressure on your major blood vessels. You also can't lay on a pregnancy belly. This means that she may have to lie on her side, and cushions will be used to make it as comfortable and supportive as possible.

Massages can be extremely beneficial to pregnant mothers, as they can help with hormone regulation. Studies show that the production of the stress hormone lessens in pregnant women who have massages once per fortnight, as it encourages the increased development of dopamine and serotonin.

They can also reduce nerve pain, as many people suffer from pains in their joints, muscles, and back throughout pregnancy. It can also decrease stress and anxiety, as well as improving circulation. In addition to all these benefits, it can also reduce swelling too. That's because the swelling is caused due to the strain on the pregnant mom's blood vessels and the extra weight they carry.

Prenatal massages are also linked with relieving symptoms of insomnia, headaches, and congestion too, which are all common pregnancy symptoms at this stage.

When seeking a therapist, you should ensure you contact a certified prenatal massage therapist that has the training needed to work with pregnant women. They will know all about positioning, the massage techniques they should use, and symptoms to watch out for such as varicose veins, blood clots, or dizziness. They'll ask your partner to answer several questions regarding health conditions, to ensure they're safe.

What Should Dad Do?

We're at month four, and things are going pretty well, but it can be difficult to intuit what's expected of you at this stage or what you can do to help her out. It's okay to ask her – she doesn't expect you to just know everything.

My friend Rob was just coming around to the idea of an unplanned pregnancy by month 4. He and his wife were just getting their careers off the ground, so they had lengthy discussions about the pregnancy in the early stages and kept it quiet. He didn't respond well, so there was conflict.

By month 4, Rob came to terms with the fact he was going to be a dad and he and his wife Claire had a plan. He went through a stage where he was hard on himself, as he felt guilty for his feelings in the early stages – he was against the pregnancy and this caused a rift in his marriage for a short time. The first ultrasound changed everything because things became real and he felt so much love for his child, hence his guilty feelings.

He went overboard trying to make things right, and even hired someone to bring them dinner every evening and cleaner to save his wife from doing these jobs, but it wasn't what she wanted and was an unnecessary spend. Other things were much more important to her, like him being involved in the pregnancy while also their relationship. On speaking to Claire, we found out what she wanted… asking her would certainly have saved Rob a few dollars.

We've got some awesome tips from Claire of what Rob could've done to help at this stage:

- Share the housework with your other half – don't let her do everything. Just join in with her and do it together (bear in mind, she may not want a cleaner or someone to cook dinner)
- Make sure you're doing the heavy lifting – she is expanding and at risk of injury, so be there to move the heavy things
- Talk through the things that are stressing her out in life and help her relax – talking and taking an interest in her life really helps and strengthens your relationship
- Encourage her to exercise and join in – she doesn't always feel motivated to exercise so join in with her

- Talk through the things you may need to do later, as she progresses in the pregnancy – her hospital bag, equipment, and clothing you may need, colors for the baby's room, and her birthing options. If you start talking about it early on, you can get it right later

- Plan a date night and ensure it's something you'll both enjoy – she wants to do something fun to make her feel normal, so taking her on a date night to do something she'll enjoy is always a winner

- Suggest looking into antenatal classes that you can attend together – she wants you to be there and take an interest in the pregnancy and birth, so book some antenatal classes together so you both know what to do or expect. Pregnancy and birth can be scary things!

Month 4 Reflection

As the pregnancy progresses, there are still things you may be thinking about, so we've put together a list of 5 of the most asked questions at this stage.

1. What happens to her body in the second trimester?

Your baby goes through a huge spurt during the second trimester which means her uterus and stomach area expand, getting bigger and bigger. While early pregnancy symptoms subside, most women feel well during this stage before the symptoms of late pregnancy appear. While mom's bump will begin to show, she also has a lot of hormonal changes to deal with too.

2. Should she be eating more food now that her body is feeding 2 people?

This is a common misconception as while you should be eating a little more, you shouldn't eat double the amount – it's not necessarily the quantity that matters, it's the quality. She should be eating healthily and should be eating around 350 calories more per day, on average, but this should be a gradual increase.

3. Should I start to feel my baby move and kick?

Mama-to-be's will feel their baby kick during the second trimester, but it's not quite time yet. Movements are usually felt between 18-20 weeks, so you've got this to look forward to next month. Exciting times are ahead!

4. What symptoms are not normal at this stage of the pregnancy?

Miscarriage risks decrease significantly in the second trimester, but if the pregnant party suffers from symptoms of bleeding or cramping, they should seek medical attention urgently, especially if this becomes severe. Such symptoms can indicate pregnancy complications, so it's best to get her checked out if this happens.

5. Is it common to pee a lot more?

An increase in the need to urinate is common throughout pregnancy, especially as the baby grows. The pregnancy is causing increased blood flow to the kidneys along with your overactive hormones, creating more urine in the body. Don't forget, the baby takes up more space as it grows too, which puts more pressure on the bladder, so feeling the need to pee regularly is normal.

Congratulations – you've graduated month 4!

If you think month 4 sounds exciting, there's so much going on as you head into month 5.

> A new baby is like the beginning of all things – wonder, hope, a dream of possibilities."
>
> — EDA LESHAN

Snuggle up close with her in bed on a night, while you can… Embrace the beginning of your parenting journey, together – it starts with pregnancy!

THE FIFTH MONTH

Congratulations! Month five is a huge milestone in pregnancy as it means that by the middle of the month, you're halfway there. At 20 weeks, you'll have your anatomy ultrasound, and your healthcare professional will confirm that your baby is the right size and that it's growing healthily. You can even find out the sex of the baby at this stage too.

This chapter will focus on development between 18-24 weeks, and we'll also talk about your baby's registry too. We'll also talk about your 20-week scan, as well as your month 5 checklist. We'll also discover some helpful tips for the dad-to-be.

Don't forget to keep taking those photographs to make your memories. Keeping a record of her cravings, the baby's first kicks, and the ultrasounds, to accompany the images of mom, dad and bump will be awesome!

Before we get to the nitty-gritty, let's look at month 5's incredible fact…

Incredible Fact #5

Babies can be born with teeth!

No, that doesn't mean they're super-human or are in fact vampires, but it can be a shock. This isn't a concern unless it disturbs feeding or becomes a choking hazard.

Generally, babies get their first tooth between months 4-7 after their birth but some babies are born with teeth, however, this is rare. When this happens, we refer to the teeth as natal teeth, but this only happens to 1 in every 2000 babies.

Your baby is already one in a million, so let's look at how they are developing throughout month 5.

Pregnancy Week 18-22

Your baby is still going through its growth spurt, and at week 18, your baby is the size of a bell pepper, but by week 22, it will be the size of a papaya.

By week 18, your baby's face will be well developed, as their ears, nose, and lips are all recognizable. Their eyebrows, eyelids, eyelashes, hair, and nails are well formed and visible on an ultrasound. Baby will also have girl or boy parts, so if you're having a boy, his genitals will be visible, and for a girl, her uterus and fallopian tubes are already in place. Their lungs are starting to develop further as their little tubes develop and at the end of these, the respiratory sack begins to appear. They have tiny blood vessels that allow you to breathe oxygen and carbon dioxide.

When the pregnancy is at week 19, all five senses are working s they've developed the nerve cells in the brain. They have already learned how to swallow and are somersaulting around the womb nicely. Your baby will be moving around regularly, and your partner may be able to feel it. It starts as a feeling of butterflies in your stomach, then it gets stronger as the baby grows.

When you're at week 20, your baby will be able to suck its thumb. This is halfway through the pregnancy, and at this stage, your ultrasound will take place and you may be able to find out the sex of your baby if you wish. Some people prefer this to be a surprise at birth.

Week 21 starts your countdown to the birth – in just 19 weeks your little one will be here. Their skin is wrinkled and quite see-through, with a tint of red because of the blood vessels. Smooth, beautiful skin will be theirs in the future. At this time, your baby's liver and spleen are producing more blood cells, and the bone marrow is well developed too. Your baby is getting its nourishment from the placenta and is also taking in small amounts of the amniotic fluid – basically, it's drinking it. Your baby has working taste buds too!

As you know, your baby is moving well, but your baby's arms and legs are more in proportion with its body now. While previously, your little one was measured from head to butt, it will now be measured from head to heel. By week 22, your baby's lungs are developing, and baby is practicing using them while in the womb. The intensity of baby moving will have increased, so your partner may alert you when movement is occurring so you can place your hand on her bump and feel it – this is such a treasured moment for you both. Your baby can you so both of you should talk and sing to her bump. Your partner will probably have quite a bump now and may choose to rub it with suitable moisturizer too, as you talk or sing. While it's a bit strange at first, don't give up, as it helps you bond with your baby. They'll find your voice soothing to them as it becomes familiar.

Creating Your Registry

It's an exciting time in pregnancy, but there's so much to consider before your little bundle of joy is here. Now would be a great time for you and your partner to sit down and create your baby registry.

A baby registry is a list of items that parents-to-be would like to receive as gifts for their new baby. They're usually purchased from a specific store, and it ensures that they get the things they need or want, while ensuring they don't get duplicate items. You can register at more than one store though, and it's often best to choose a location that fits in with your family and friends, although with online stores, location is not an issue.

Your friends and family can then go to the store to buy your baby a gift where you are registered, they can then ask to look at your registry and select an item to purchase. The store will then mark this off your list. It also works similarly, if you opt for online.

It isn't always easy to construct a baby registry, so we've provided you with some ideas below, to get you started:

- Items for bathing (bathtub, washcloths, soft towels with a hood, baby shampoo and conditioner, simple bath toys)

- Bedding (crib mattress, waterproof mattress protector, fitted sheets)
- Swaddling blankets
- Clothing – you will need lots of clothing, including:
    - Elastic-waist trousers or leggings
    - Pajamas with feet
    - Socks
    - Short-sleeved onesies
    - Long-sleeved onesies
    - Sun hats
    - Soft hats
    - Hospital outfit
    - Soft-soled shoes or booties for babies
    - Bathing suits
    - Snow suits
    - Scratch mitts
    - Sweaters, zip-up hoodies, or cardigans
    - Laundry detergent – baby-safe
- Feeding (bibs, burp cloths, breast pump, milk freezer bags, nursing pillow, nursing bras, baby bottles, bottle brushes, nipple cream, nursing cover, highchair)
- Changing or diapering (diaper pail, diaper cream, baby wipes, diapers, cotton balls)
- Nursery furniture (crib, rocking chair, changing table, baby monitor, baby books, baskets, or storage bins)
- Baby medical supplies (thermometer, nail trimmer for baby, suction bulb, saline nasal drops, teething gel)

- Toys (play mats, teething toys, swing or bouncer, rattles, or maracas)
- Items for travel (stroller, stroller bunting to protect baby from the rain and cold, car seat for newborns, diaper bag, portable changing mat, travel crib)

You should avoid adding cot bumpers, pillows, and stuffed toys, as this goes against safe sleeping practices. You also don't need dressy clothes or tons of toys either.

There are many places for you to start your online baby registry. We've come up with a list of our top 7:

- Walmart baby registry
- Pottery Barn baby registry
- Ikea baby registry
- Amazon baby registry
- Target baby registry
- Bed Bath and Beyond baby registry
- The Tot baby registry (Eco-friendly)

The baby registry is great because you and your partner get to do this together, and it's a great way to build up excitement.

Month Five To-do List

Your month 5 to-do list is here, and no doubt, you're doing great so far. Keep going – you're more than halfway there.

- Keep checking that she's taking her prenatal vitamins – they're really important!
- While she won't be suffering from the symptoms of early pregnancy, there are some symptoms she still may have. You can help her by helping to ease her symptoms:
  a. Heartburn – this is caused by hormonal changes and the baby pressing on your stomach. To avoid this, your partner should eat healthily, change eating and drinking habits, and keep upright. They should also avoid alcohol and caffeine, and they should stop smoking. To ease this, your partner can take certain antacids or alginates, available over the counter. If symptoms persist, they can see their doctor who will provide them with further advice and prescribe some medication.
  b. Back pain – this is another common pregnancy symptom, due to the ligaments stretching and becoming softer, preparing for labor. She should certainly avoid lifting heavy objects and use pillows to support her back when she sits or lays. Sometimes, back pain eases if you take back care classes, wear flat shoes, or have a warm bath. A prenatal massage (discussed in chapter 4) could help too. She should contact her healthcare practitioner if she is in the second or third trimester, and back pain is not subsiding, if she has a fever or bleeding, or pain when she pees to accompany her back pain, or if she has pains

under her ribs or in her sides. If she loses the feeling in her legs, bum, or genitals, she should seek urgent medical help.

c. Fast heartbeat – sometimes, the heart rate of a pregnant woman may increase, which could be due to the anticipation of the little one arriving, but it can also be because her heart is working harder. If her heart rate stays elevated for a long time, or if she has breathing difficulties, she should speak to her healthcare provider. She may need rest, so take care of her.

d. Leg cramps – often occur at night, in the lower legs. To prevent such symptoms, staying hydrated, massaging the calf, and maintaining regular exercise, can all help with leg cramps. She could also try an icepack or take a warm bath. It's also believed that taking a magnesium supplement and making sure you take adequate calcium can also prevent leg cramps. When cramps occur, she should stretch out the calf muscle too, to ease the pain.

e. Swollen hands and feet – it's perfectly normal for her to get some swelling, gradually, but this can get to the point in which it's uncomfortable. To reduce this, she should wear comfortable shoes and avoid standing for long periods. Exercising the ankles and feet, or walking, can also help. She should make sure she drinks plenty of water too, as this helps rid the body of excess water. If you notice that the swelling comes on suddenly or increases, or you get a headache, vision issues, pain in the lower ribs, or vomiting, then you should seek medical attention as soon as possible.

- Take a babymoon - a babymoon is like a honeymoon. It's a vacation to help you celebrate the pregnancy and give you some time together before your little one arrives. There are no strict rules here, so think about whether you're going to book a week away or just a few days. If you don't feel like it, you could have a staycation, but block out the outside world and focus on you two. This will allow you to reconnect when you've been focused on the baby. The second, or early third trimester is a great time to do this, but remember, you should make it as memorable as possible so arrange this before she feels too uncomfortable. Make it fun, and enjoy your quality time, but ensure it's a stress-free and relaxing time for your partner. This whole experience should be captured, so don't forget to make memories by taking pictures to add to your collection. Having a baby is one of life's great transitions, so a baby moon will help you both mentally prepare and recharge.

So... Are You Finding Out the Gender? Everything You Need to Know About the Anatomy Scan

You'll be super-excited that your anatomy scan is on the horizon, and you can go with your partner when they get this scan – it's a great experience for your both to share. This is usually carried out between weeks 18-21, and it looks at the development of your baby physically. You can get a 2d image in black and white, however, some people opt for a 3d scan which can cost extra. To get this scan, she needs to give her permission.

The scan looks at the baby's bones, hers, face, abdomen, brain, and spinal cord, and the person conducting the scan can look for 11 rare medical conditions, including anencephaly, cleft lip, open spina bifida, lethal skeletal dysplasia, Edward's syndrome, Patau's syndrome, bilateral renal agenesis, exomphalos, diaphragmatic hernia, and gastroschisis.

You can find out the sex of your baby at this scan, but it's best to ask the person scanning you before they begin scanning, so they know they check this if they can. A colleague of mine was desperate to know the sex of their baby. His wife wanted a surprise, but after some persuasion, he persuaded her. They found out they were having a boy and so, they bought a blue pram, painted the bedroom baby blue and white, and bought blue clothing items. They told their family and friends that they were having a boy, but to their surprise, when his wife gave birth, they had a girl…

Although the scans are pretty accurate these days, there is a chance that the person scanning you can get it wrong from time to time. They are typically accurate, but they do usually come with a disclaimer explaining that it's not always accurate, so just bear that in mind.

This scan is recommended; however, it is a choice and is not mandatory. If the scan shows something, the staff will double-check this and explain to you what's happening. If they think further tests are necessary then they will talk to you about this, and you can also talk about this with your doctor or midwife.

Finally, it's important to add that it's okay to ask questions before or after the scan too. Some practitioners don't mind if you ask them throughout. Most of all, enjoy this experience with you, your partner, and your little one!

How to be an Awesome Dad-to-be and Partner in Month 5

Throughout month 5, we've talked about her, so it's important to switch the focus onto her a little more. Of course, there's the scan and other experiences to look forward to, but it's time to enjoy your alone time. Let's look at six key ways in which you can become not only an awesome dad but also an awesome partner.

She could be feeling tired and it's normal to have swelling, vaginal discharge, or occasional dizziness. She does need to keep an eye on these symptoms as if the swelling is sudden, the dizziness is regular, or if the vaginal discharge is smelly or discolored, she should seek medical advice. Keep an eye on her and ensure she rests well. Be sure to ask her how she's feeling, if she has any concerns, and encourage her to speak to a doctor if necessary.

If your other half has hip pain at night, invest in a giant body pillow, and encourage her to sleep on her side, with the pillow between her knees. This will help to ease her symptoms.

Remember to arrange that babymoon. It's the perfect time for you to celebrate the pregnancy and reconnect!

She needs you on her side, more than ever, both during the pregnancy and when the baby arrives. Lots of people will be coming forward and providing parenting advice, and while mama will take it on board initially, it gets tiresome. Mama has her instincts and if she ever needs help and support, she'll ask for it. Too much advice can confuse and irritate – things change so much, so sometimes information from others is not accurate anyway. Talk about the rules you're setting as she gets later in her pregnancy, and the rules you'll set when baby is here.

She's worried about everything from childbirth to looking after and feeding the baby. All you can do is be as supportive as you can – mama knows you can't fix everything but offer her time to talk things through to prevent anxiety building.

While sex won't harm the baby, it doesn't mean that your partner will enjoy it, nor does it mean she wants to avoid it. The only way you'll know is to talk about it with her but you should consider her sexual needs first. Some women lose interest in sex, while others want more than they did before.

Month Five Questions

It's time to reflect on month 5, so let's look at some of the most common questions:

1. Are babymoons just for first-time parents?

No, they're certainly not. It's just a way for you to come together and celebrate the pregnancy while being able to relax, reconnect and refresh before your new baby arrives. If you're already an experienced parent, you'll already know how difficult it is to snatch a few hours alone once your bundle of joy is here.

2. *When does the second trimester end?*

The second trimester ends at 27 weeks, so your third trimester starts at the beginning of week 28.

3. *Should we count the fetal kicks?*

It's not necessary during weeks 18-22. We count the fetal kicks to measure if you're exerting yourself or not moving enough. This is something that's usually measured at 26-28 weeks. You want the baby to move normally, so typically, this is 10 times within a 2-hour period. If it's more, you could be doing too much, but if it's less, you may want to move a little more.

4. *Why does the 20-week scan examine the baby's heart?*

The scan checks that the heart is the correct size and looks for congenital heart defects in the baby. If they catch such a thing prenatal, they can ensure your baby gets the best care throughout your pregnancy and on their arrival. If you have any pressing questions, don't be afraid to ask. Sometimes it's best to come up with a list before you go.

Now that you've made it to the end of month 5, you're counting down the months, weeks, and days until your little one is here. Exciting times are ahead as we move into month 6.

THE SIXTH MONTH

When you reach the sixth month of pregnancy, it's all systems go. If you thought month 5 was exciting, we're going to talk about gender reveals and baby showers throughout month 6.

> It won't be long until you are here,
> I can't wait to hold you near.
> We'll kiss your head, stroke your hair,
> Hold your hand, and show we care.

In this chapter, we'll explore baby's development during weeks 23-27, and we'll also talk through the all-important to-do list, before focusing on baby kicking. After that, we're going to talk through picking a name before we provide you with some helpful tips.

You're on the home stretch now, so just a couple more months to go. But before we continue, let's look at our incredible month 6 fact…

Incredible Fact #6

Did you know a woman's voice can change during her pregnancy? That doesn't mean she will suddenly start talking in a new accent or dialect, it means her pitch changes, which is believed to be down to her hormone changes. Hormones are known to increase pitch around the time of ovulation but decrease significantly during menopause, however, there isn't a lot of research confirming that pregnancy changes this too. If hormones are linked with voice pitch changes, it's certainly plausible that pregnancy would cause this!

Pregnancy Weeks 23-27

Your partner and you have made it to the sixth month of pregnancy, and by the 23rd week, the baby is as big as a grapefruit. Your baby is still pretty skinny, as the weight seems to come towards the end of the pregnancy. Their vision, hearing, and grip are getting better, and their lungs and nose are more functional.

Your baby is starting to appear more baby-like. The fetus is fiercely working on developing your little one's brain, and you may notice that they become more active following a meal or drink. Some women notice that their baby is more active at night, which means she could miss some vital sleep.

By week 24, she'll be glowing, due to her ever-changing pregnancy. The lungs of your baby are growing rapidly so that they can ensure they have enough space for oxygen and carbon dioxide. Your baby will have started to gain weight, even though they're still skinny.

By week 25, your baby has developed its startle reflex which means it'll jump when spooked. Their baby fat is increasing, and their wrinkly appearance is changing. If your baby is born with hair, the texture starts to appear around now. Your baby is now over a foot long!

When the pregnancy is at 26 weeks, your baby has tiny fingernails, but just remember when baby arrives, they'll be jagged and quite sharp. The baby is still practicing swallowing by taking in small amounts of amniotic fluid, and this action helps them develop healthy lungs. Their brain wave activity is kicking in and their eyes are open, and their little eyelashes are growing. They'll soon wrap you around their finger when your cute little baby is born.

Towards the end of the month, your baby will begin to recognize your voice as they can hear you clearly, and they will have grown to the size of a head of cabbage. She could have a gymnast, a soccer player, or a dancer in there, as they'll enjoy moving around to tone their muscles. If you feel regular jerks in your belly, it could mean your baby is hiccupping. They're going to keep growing, developing, and building up their baby weight, to prepare them for birth. The end of the 27th week marks the end of the second trimester.

Announcing the Gender

When you've had your 20-week scan, if you've learned the gender of your baby, you and your partner have a decision to make…

Do you reveal the gender to friends and family?

We have several decisions to make when we're becoming parents many people will probably ask you if you're having a boy or girl and if you've chosen a name. Sharing this is down to you and your partner – it's your preference.

Some people choose to keep the news quiet, while others go all out by having a gender reveal party. They are certainly increasing in popularity.

A gender reveal is basically how you tell the world the gender of your baby and some do this in crazy, fun, or exciting ways. For example, some people get a cake and cut it open, and the color of the inside of the cake reveals the baby's gender. For example, blue for a boy and pink for a girl. Others get a party popper, or a pop a balloon, but inside is blue or pink confetti. You can use baby clothes to reveal the gender, or ribbons cutely by wrapping up her belly or adding a cute ribbon to your scan image. You could have a bouquet of balloons in a large box, create biscuits (or other sweet treats)

The reasons why parents decide to do a gender reveal, and this includes:

- It can be easier to come up with a name
- They don't want a neutral nursery, they want it to be colorful and fun, but they want to choose colors, or a theme based on gender
- Some people hope for a specific gender, so if you don't get what you expect, it allows you time to get used to the idea
- It allows your family to share in your joy or excitement

- You can enjoy the reactions you get from others, before the birth
- It allows you to prepare in advance for your baby's arrival
- Others can choose more personal gifts

There are many reasons why people choose not to reveal the gender of their baby too. Just remember, this is a choice. A friend of mine and his wife decided to do a gender reveal and it was great. They'd picked a name out for their daughter and shared this with a select few. His wife's friend was pregnant too, and she had her baby first. Unfortunately, she used the exact name they'd chosen. He told me how upset his wife was, and they contemplated using the same name but felt their experience was ruined and she was devastated. He took her on their babymoon and while they took this time together, they figured out a new name that was much iconic for their family. Needless to say, they kept this one under wraps. Of course, most gender reveal parties are fun and work out well. Just ensure that when it comes to the name you choose, you only tell those you trust completely – your nearest and dearest.

Gender reveals are great, so it's certainly something to get excited about. In the meantime, let's consider the important things you need to do.

Month Six To-Do List

Your month 6 to-do list is waiting for you. With just a few more months to go, it's time to get cracking.

1. Is she still taking her prenatal vitamins? Remember how important they are and keep encouraging her to take them.

2. Watch out for symptoms and help her ease them, such as:

    a. Hemorrhoids – creams for hemorrhoids are available over the counter, so if symptoms persist, you can pick her some cream up from your local pharmacist. Just encourage her to use it as it can really ease symptoms, but if symptoms persist, seek medical advice.

    b. Restless legs – this is positional discomfort, which can also lead to cramps and sore muscles. Use ice or heat to ease the pain, but you should never use rubs or gels that are unsafe during pregnancy. Sometimes caffeine and smoking cause this, so avoid these things. She could also try exercise, meditation, and massage, to help ease this symptom. It may be a good idea to seek medical attention if there are swelling or signs of varicose veins.

    c. Fast-growing or extra hair – she might notice that the hair on her head is thicker, and this is due to the changes in hormones. Encourage her to enjoy this. She wants to hear about it if she looks good! Sometimes, this change causes extra body hair on the face and body, and, likely she won't like this symptom. Be sensitive and supportive about this. If it's bugging her, there are safe methods of hair removal, such as tweezing, waxing, and threading, to consider.

d. False labor (AKA Braxton Hicks) – she may feel a tightening or cramping in the stomach area, but this soon passes and is nothing to worry about. It doesn't mean she's ready to give birth, it's simply toning the muscles in her uterus and helping her cervix prepare for birth. As she progresses through her pregnancy, towards the end, they can occur more frequently. Some people report Braxton Hicks within the middle of the second trimester, but they are more common now she's in her third. They are different from labor because they only last for around 30 seconds and occur 1-2 times per hour, they are irregular, they often stop if she changes position or activity, and while they are uncomfortable, they are not painful. Having a bath or shower can ease them, and they do not signal that your cervix is starting to thin or open. Real labor is more intense and regular, and the contractions last longer and get stronger, often worsening when you walk. They do signify her cervix thinning and opening, and last between 30-70 seconds. If she is unable to differentiate between which one is happening (which does happen), you should seek medical advice to ease her worry. They may offer an examination to put her mind at rest. If it is Braxton Hicks, her symptoms can be eased by having a warm bath, taking a walk, laying down and resting, or by having a massage.

    e.   Dental health – if she hasn't been for a dental check-up, she should certainly get herself booked in. She should ensure she's brushing her teeth at least twice per day, and she should also be flossing. She is at risk of developing gum issues, such as gingivitis or periodontitis, which puts her and the baby at risk of preeclampsia or premature birth.

3.   Take care of yourself – now this book has focused a lot on baby and mama, but you also need to take care of yourself. Now is the best time to do this, before baby arrives, but some people choose to do this much earlier. Make sure you've got your leave and any vacation time sorted in time for the baby's arrival. You also need to set yourself up for financial stability if you haven't already. The first step is to figure out how you're doing now. *What are you earning, and do you have enough to comfortably keep your baby?* Try to cut down on your credit cards and loans, and check your credit file to ensure it's correct. Talk to your employer about paternity, maternity, and any other benefits the company offers – this could even include childcare vouchers. Consider how solid you are financially and talk to your partner about this. *Will they be working once the child is born?* It's also good to ensure you both have life insurance policies and produce a will, stating who will care for your child in the absence of you and your partner, as it's good to clarify this. You should also consider how you can make savings, to take care of your baby. You should also think about their healthcare coverage and

college fund too. As well as all the financial stuff, make sure you're well rested and feeling fit and healthy.

4. *Did you sign up for those antenatal classes we mentioned?* If you didn't now is the time. you could do Lamaze classes which take a natural and healthy approach to birth, without the use of medical interventions or medicines. The Bradley method, which consists of a husband-coached birth, again, is a natural birth but allows you to coach your partner through this, but also helps you to prepare, just in case an emergency cesarean is required. The Alexander technique eases her pain by giving her freedom and flexibility, balance, movement, and coordination. It's an education process that can help aid recovery from childbirth, while also improving comfort in pregnancy, increasing the quality of pushing during delivery, and helping to ease any comfort she experiences from nursing. You can speak to your doctor or any other pregnancy practitioners that are involved in the care of your partner and their child to find out where these birthing classes are taking place.

5. Consider infant CPR classes. They can be a great skill to learn which can save lives just in case your baby chokes or stops breathing for some reason. Your midwife or other pregnancy-related healthcare professional will be able to signpost you to some local classes.

6. Remember to sing and talk to the baby. Your baby recognizes dad and mom's distinct voices and will become more familiar with them. You can soothe them by singing lullabies,

which may even help them feel at ease when they are born. This can enhance their well-being and help them feel safe.

There are many ways that dad can enjoy the pregnancy too, so remember to do this. Sometimes we spend so much time worrying about other things, we forget to enjoy the things that matter. Let's talk about one of those treasured moments – like when your baby kicks.

Feeling Baby Kick

We've talked a little about baby kicking in chapter 5, but dads often react in different ways to this. Some are excited, others are filled with emotion and love, while others are overwhelmed and even sometimes, you may feel a bit freaked out.

Mom has been feeling the baby kick from somewhere between 18-22 weeks, but it starts with the feelings of butterflies in the stomach and then intensifies. By 24 weeks, you will probably be able to feel the baby when it's active.

To do this, ask your partner to alert you when the baby is being a gymnast, and ask them to put your hand on their belly. If you're lucky, you'll feel it. This is a special moment for you and your partner, it makes everything seem more real.

Different responses are normal, so there's no right or wrong here. Enjoy the experience – you could even document it or take a picture or video. Respond in a way that feels natural to you – some people are so surprised when baba kicks, especially if they've never experienced this yet.

You and your partner may want to take some time when choosing a name, so let's move on and discuss this next.

Picking a Name

Picking a name is an extremely important task for you and mama. Some people opt for more popular baby names, while others want a more unique name. One of the crucial things to consider when you name your baby is whether the name allows for growth – for example, your baby will eventually be grown up, and then elderly, *so is it a name they can take with them or adapt?*

Some people want to choose a name that honors a family member, which is great. Many of my friends have lost a parent or grandparent and want to honor them in some way through the name of their baby. There's also the possibility of a nickname, for example, the name Abigail can be nicknamed Abbie, and the name Christopher can be shortened to Chris. Some people find that they like the longer name, but dislike the nickname, and vice-versa. It's something you both need to consider, but in some ways, a name that allows a nickname means more flexibility for the child in the future.

Your baby has got to live with the name you give them, so consider if you would like that name too. That doesn't mean a child shouldn't have a unique name, just think about it carefully. Often, mom and dad struggle to come up with a name they both like, so you may need to compromise. Contemplate using the names as middle names and decide on a name you both agree on, allow one parent to choose the name of the first child, but the other will choose the name of the second child (if you plan on having more than one child), combine the names in some way or avoid using them altogether. Some people even take a vote, but you may need to involve your friends and family if there are only the two of you.

Now for more fun…

To baby shower, or to not baby shower?

Baby Shower Fun

Now there is a stigma surrounding baby showers and it's a popular belief that dads don't go. This doesn't have to be true – it's up to the host. Some prefer to have a little soirée of their own – while moms head into the sitting room, dads head into the kitchen for a good-old catch-up, but there are no hard and fast rules when it comes to baby showers, so it's entirely up to the host or the parent preferences.

But what exactly is baby shower etiquette?

Traditionally, baby showers were for women only and some people still prefer it that way. However, modern society is constantly changing, and not everyone wants to follow tradition, as they want to do their own thing. The truth is, it's a decision you can make together – but be sure to let her friends know, in case they want to arrange one for her.

Ultimately, the baby shower is about mama and baby. There's no reason why you should go or shouldn't go but if you don't, there's no reason why you can't do something with the boys, for example, have a few beers, a barbecue or order pizza, and maybe even watch the game. There are lots of things dads can do, *so why not throw your own shower?*

1. Have a get-together with your bros, but bring dad a gift – what about a daddy survival kit? Baked goods? A nappy-changing guide? There are some weird, wonderful, and fun ideas out there – you will have a great time!

2. Practice changing diapers… BLINDFOLDED!

3. Have a stroller race – no babies please, just a doll! This is a relay race and to win, you need two strollers. Set up an obstacle course in the garden so that the racers can take turns in teams following the route. To make it difficult, use hoses, ladders, chairs, shovels, and anything else you find in the garden.

Now we've thought about some fun things for you to do, at your baby shower, let's talk through some helpful tips for dads, to ensure you're still in the good books with your baby mama.

Helpful Tips for Dad

There's so much going on in month 6, but if there are some things she'll be doing right or feeling right now, that you can help with. If you want to be supportive and helpful, recognizing the three points below will certainly help:

1. Don't pressurize her! - There are certain things she'll want to do and not want to do. She may not yet know if she wants to reveal the baby's gender, or she may not be ready to choose

a name. Nor may she be ready to make baby shower plans – she may want to talk to you and her friends, first. Pressure makes her feel more emotional, and her hormones are already crazy. Give her some time and space, listen to her, and be patient. It will all work out!

2. There's a living being inside of her! - It's quite overwhelming. It eats her food, moves around, and makes her uncomfortable, making her body and mind act out of character. Show your interest in her and the amazing experience of pregnancy when the baby moves. Remember to talk to your little one and ask your partner if you can track the progress together. Knowing how big baby is as we talk about in this book can help you be part of the journey.

3. Nesting is something she takes seriously - You probably won't get it, but when she's rushing around and possibly nagging, trying to motivate you to get things prepared for the birth, it's her time to get things ready. It's like an intuition inside that tells her she must get it done before she's too tired or gives birth. While it's currently early for her to give birth, she'll still have so much on her mind and there'll be so much she wants to do. Nesting typically comes on in waves, and it's a stressful feeling. One stressful comment from you or even an eye roll will cause conflict. You can support her by asking her what she wants you to do or if there's anything you can do to help. You should also make refreshments and encourage rest in between.

Month Six Q&A

It's time for you to reflect on what we've talked about in this chapter, by focusing on some of the most frequently asked questions for parents, when they're six months into their pregnancy.

1. Do I have to do the whole gender reveal thing? My partner is excited but it's stressing me out.

Absolutely not! You are not forced into doing anything you don't want to do. You and your partner are in control of the situation, so talk and listen to one another. Talk about why it's wanted, and why it isn't. There's no rush, so give each other a bit of time to process the gender yourself.

2. We've finally decided on the first and middle names for our baby, however, my partner and I aren't married. How do we choose which surname to use?

There are always compromises to be made when we're parenting. Some people prefer to go with the traditional ways in which they name their child after the father. It's not uncommon for a woman to want to be involved in the surname, which is why we see a lot of double-barreled names. Others plan to get married, decide on which surname to take or they'll combine the two, so they all have the same family name. It's down to you both to decide, so listen to each other and see if there's a compromise that you can both come to. Listen to both sides – you may come to an amicable solution.

3. I'm worried about my partner, she's happy one minute, snappy the next, and then, out of nowhere, she cries. What should I do?

In this first instance, talk to your partner about how they are feeling. While it's important not to gloss over issues, it's also important to make sure she's taken seriously. We will never fully understand others, so it's impossible to know exactly how she feels, but try to support her and help her unwind. Put yourself in her shoes and listen to her venting. Encourage her to rest and talk to her about how she feels – try your best to understand. If you are concerned, seek professional advice. You could start with her doctor or midwife.

TOP TIP

She wants you to be SPONTANEOUS from time to time. Sure, she's tired, but she'd love a surprise. If you think she'd go out – take her out for dinner. If you think she'd like to relax, book her in for a prenatal massage. If you think she wants to stay home, eat in, bring her flowers, and dig out or hire her favorite movie.

You're officially moving to trimester 3 – *can you believe it?* Just the final 12 weeks before the baby is here! Let's talk about what happens in month 7, next.

7 THE SEVENTH MONTH

You've made it to the third and final trimester of pregnancy – it's all hands on deck from now on. In this chapter, we'll talk about everything you need to know when it comes to month 7, and in addition to this, we're covering pre-eclampsia, packing for your hospital visit (if applicable), and we're going to delve deep into Braxton Hicks contraction, versus the real deal.

There's so much to talk about and so little time, as your baby will be growing and developing well. We'll also talk through some of the symptoms your pregnant partner may be experiencing throughout this month, as well as putting together our monthly to-do list, so you know exactly what you need to do.

We've also got some great tips for you this month – but just imagine, in 2 months, your newborn will be here!

But before we get to that point, it's time for another fun fact…

Incredible Fact #7

Your unborn baby can taste certain foods whilst still in the womb. They detect the flavor, by swallowing the amniotic fluid every day, and this includes tastes of what the mother has eaten. Their sense of taste first develops at 8 weeks as this is the time during gestation when the first taste buds appear.

This means babies have already experienced similar taste patterns to their mothers long before they start eating their food.

Pregnancy Weeks 28-32

The third trimester is an amazing time. It's the last phase before the baby arrives, and during this time, your baby rapidly develops. By the beginning of month seven, your baby is the size of a head of lettuce – imagine carrying a head of lettuce around with you, everywhere you go.

When babies first develop, they are long and thin, but from now (and particularly over the next few weeks), they will start getting fatter. This isn't a negative thing! Your baby needs to do this.

At 28 weeks, your baby dreams and we know this because of the baby's REM (rapid eye movements). Your baby can now blink – up until now their eyes have been closed but they now have little eyelashes too. Your baby may even be making funny faces by sticking out their tongue too. Although, we're not 100% sure why this happens! Your baby probably weighs just over 2.2 pounds (1 kilogram), and is around 15 inches (or 38 centimeters) long, from head to toe. Their senses are also functional at this age, and your baby's brain and nervous system are developing nicely. The nervous system is starting to control breathing movements which strengthens the lungs and body temperature.

At 29 weeks, your baby begins to smile, but this is usually while they are sleeping. They have less space now and are cramped in the womb, so the kicks you were feeling will feel more like jabs. As they put on more weight, their wrinkles become less apparent. By the time your baby reaches 30 weeks, its skin will begin to color as the skin cells begin to produce melanin, although your baby's permanent skin tone won't be fully developed until they are around 6 months old. They will now have more hair on their head, but less hair elsewhere on their body – the body hair will mostly fall out before birth anyway. They can now open their eyes wide and see dim shapes.

By week 31, your baby's brain connections are developing rapidly. They should develop billions of them before birth. Baby can also process information through the brain and pick up signals, that are triggered by the senses. Your baby is starting to snooze for longer, too, and this could develop into patterns that you recognize – they can have periods of rest, wakefulness, and times of movement. Many often enjoy sucking their thumbs and pedaling their feet. Their eyes can expand or constrict, which allows them to let in less light, or more if needed.

By 32 weeks, with only 8 weeks left to go, your baby is as large as a cantaloupe. They weigh approximately 3.75 pounds (or 1.7 kilograms) and are around 16.5 inches (or 42 centimeters) long. They are practicing their breathing by inhaling amniotic fluid, which allows them to use and strengthen their lungs. Your baby's skin has now transformed from being transparent, to opaque, and their major organs are also fully developed, but not the lungs, as they take a little longer. Baby can recognize the day and night and may be developing sleep and wake cycles that are becoming more consistent.

Now we've talked about baby, it's time to talk about something more serious – Pre-eclampsia! This is a condition that all pregnant women, their partners, and their families or friends should be aware of.

Understanding Pre-eclampsia

Pre-eclampsia is a serious blood pressure condition that can appear throughout pregnancy, usually after 20 weeks. It complicates up to 8% of pregnancies, worldwide, and can be very serious for mom and baby, so this condition must be treated by a healthcare professional. This is something that pregnant women and their partners should be aware of as it can even, in some cases be fatal. Depending on its severity, it could mean that your baby is delivered early, however, treatment includes taking medications to lower your blood pressure, and it needs to be carefully monitored to ensure any complications that arise are managed.

Pre-eclampsia can cause numerous complications throughout pregnancy, such as fetal growth restrictions, preterm birth, placental abruption, heart issues, organ damage, eclampsia (onset of seizures or coma), and HELLP syndrome (which is the destruction of red blood cells). To keep mom and baby safe, the earlier it's spotted, the better.

While the cause of pre-eclampsia is unknown, many factors contribute to this. It's believed that this condition begins in the placenta and is linked to blood vessels that have not developed properly. This means that the blood is unable to circulate effectively, and as a result, this increases the mother's blood pressure. Those that have pre-eclampsia often show high levels of protein in their urine and have high blood pressure.

Certain conditions that put a pregnant woman at a higher risk of developing pre-eclampsia, including:

- Pregnancies with more than one baby
- Diabetes before pregnancy
- Kidney disease
- Use of in vitro fertilization
- Hypertension prior to pregnancy
- Pre-eclampsia in a previous pregnancy
- Autoimmune disorders

Women who are overweight, over the age of 35, have had complications throughout a previous pregnancy, or if it has been over 10 years since the previous pregnancy, are at moderate risk of developing this. If it's your first pregnancy with your current partner then you should keep an eye out, especially if there is a family history of pre-eclampsia in mom or dad.

You can't exactly prevent pre-eclampsia, however, if your partner is at high risk, their doctor may recommend medication, however, it's important to discuss this with your doctor first. It's also important to make as many healthy choices as possible, especially if you've previously had this or are at an increased risk.

Common symptoms of pre-eclampsia include:

- Blurry vision
- Swelling in your face and hands
- Sensitivity to light
- Headaches
- Dark spots appearing in your vision
- Shortness of breath
- Abdominal pain on the right side
- Symptoms of seizure-like convulsing or twitching

If your partner gets any of the symptoms above, it's time to call your doctor. You should contact them immediately – don't wait – or simply go to the nearest emergency hospital department. Don't underestimate how serious this condition can develop.

You and your partner mustn't ignore these symptoms, as more serious symptoms of pre-eclampsia (if it goes undetected) are:

- Fluid on your lungs
- Low blood platelet levels
- Hypertension emergency
- Decreased urine production
- Decreased liver or kidney function

If your partner's symptoms are more serious this is dangerous for her and the baby so they must seek medical help immediately. They'll likely be admitted to hospital as they will need urgent medical attention and regular monitoring.

Now that we've covered the serious (but extremely important) pre-eclampsia, it's time to talk about packing for the hospital. That's right, it's time to pack because your little bundle of joy will be here before you know it!

Packing for the Hospital

There's so much to think about when packing for the hospital. There's not just mom to think about, there's also baby and dad too. You all need at least the essentials, so best to prepare in advance. That way, if you need to rush off to the hospital urgently, everything is ready just to grab.

It's best to start getting your bag ready during the seventh month, to ensure you're well-prepared. If you throw some things into a bag last minute, you'll likely forget something important, so it's much less stressful to get things ready in advance.

A few years ago, a work colleague of mine got called out of work as his wife had gone into early labor. They weren't expecting this and were completely unprepared, so he was relied upon to go pack what they needed... She provided him with a vague list of nightwear, something to travel home in after the birth, things for the baby, which she'd put in the bottom of the wardrobe. Of course, this was always going to end in disaster...

While he remembered most of the things for baby, he didn't grab the nappies, but wait, because that's not the best part...

He also forgot his wife's underwear. Oh, and *what do you think he packed for her return journey from the hospital?*

Only her skinny jeans!

He didn't tell us any of this, but his wife brought the baby in to meet everyone at work a few weeks later and was quick to let us all know that she had to call on her sister to save the day.

As much as we laugh about this now, I probably wouldn't have had a clue what to pack when it came to my first child if it wasn't for his wife sharing the story about this mishap. It prompted me to find out exactly what we needed, after all, I didn't want my partner heading to my workplace telling stories about my mishaps.

The best thing to do when packing for hospital is to talk to your partner and work together to get everything you, her, and the baby need – there may also be some home comforts she wants to add – but look at the checklist below, just for mama!

- Comfortable clothes – she needs clothes she's going to be comfortable in, so non-restrictive clothing is a must. Her comfort is key to her recovery. This includes things, such as:
    - A supportive or nursing bra if she plans on breast-feeding
    - A nightgown, or pajama set (at least 2). Some people opt for nursing-friendly nightwear
    - Slipper socks
    - Slip-on shoes
    - Suitable underwear

- o Comfortable pants such as joggers, or postpartum leggings
  - o Baggy T-shirts, or tops
- A robe – having a comfortable robe is a relief, because she can use it after her shower, or if she's cold, while she's up nursing, and it's soothing because it's just really warm and cozy

- Her birth plan – women are usually encouraged to create a birth plan for their baby with their midwife or doctor. You will likely know or be involved in this too. This is something you should take with you, and bring more than one copy if you can. Make sure you or your partner show this to the labor nurse as you may need to highlight any key points raised in your plan

- Toiletries – these are items she certainly needs, so it's important not to forget these. She will need shampoo, or maybe dry shampoo, her hairbrush, toothpaste, a toothbrush, face wipes, bands for her hair, and deodorant. Don't forget glasses or contacts too if she wears them.

- Snacks and drinks – be sure to pack some healthy drinks and snacks to keep you going. A reusable water bottle is extremely useful, and you need quick snacks such as dried fruit, pretzels, and bars, for example:

- An extended cell phone charging cord – labor can be a long haul, and it's likely that you and your partner will want to keep your family and friends up-t0-date when it comes to the birth of your baby. You'll also want to capture moments by taking videos or pictures and chatting with your family. Taking an extended cell phone charger helps to ensure you can charge your cell as hospitals are notorious for being far away from electrical outlets

- Nipple cream – if she's breastfeeding, it's likely that her nipples will be extremely sore, so the nipple cream is essential!

- Pillows – some women prefer to take some comforts, such as their pillow. It can set them at ease as it's something they are used to, and they know it will be comfortable

- Bath towel – again, it's suggested that she may want her bath towel too. The hospital towels are sometimes rough, therefore bringing her own gives her comfort

- Portable Bluetooth speaker (with her playlist) – playing music is how some women make it through labor. Labor can be grueling, and music can be both relaxing and motivating. Make sure she has plenty of feel-good or relaxing songs on her list as labor can last for longer than a day. Some people prefer silence, while others prefer to have options

- Postpartum care products, such as adult diapers or pads – while the hospital will generally be able to hook you up with pads and mesh underwear, some women prefer to bring their own. Many women find adult diapers more secure, and they may also need breast pads too. A perineal spray is recommended too, to ease pain in that area

- Optional items – some women prefer some other things too, to help them through labor, or just after birth. This could include:
    - A portable fan

- o A diffuser – to make the room smell like a spa
- o Magazines or books
- o Her baby book for during or after the birth

This list is flexible, so talk to her, and ask her if there are any other things she wants or needs. Remember, this list is just for her, so next, it's baba's turn.

For your baby, you should pack:

- A baby changing bag that includes:
  - o Diapers – make sure they're for newborns
  - o Water wipes
  - o A portable diaper changing mat
  - o Washcloths – for all babies wash needs, including cleaning them during a diaper change
- Breast pump and bottles (just in case)
- Swaddle blankets – depending on the weather when your baby is born
- Breathable blankets – for layers when leaving the hospital
- Clothing – it's best to pack plenty if you are unsure how long you'll be in hospital for. Some people are only in for 24 hours or less, in which case you will need:
  - o At least two sleepsuits – full-length arms and legs
  - o At least two all-in-ones, short-sleeved, fastening undershirt suits
  - o Two pairs of socks or booties
  - o A knitted hat or cap
  - o A cardigan or sweater
  - o A 'going home' outfit

- o A sleep sack – in case you need to stay in overnight
  - o Bibs – at least 5 bibs will be needed, possibly more
  - o Scratch mitts – 2-3 pairs of mittens
  - o A hooded towel
- Baby toiletries:
  - o Soap or body wash for babies
  - o Shampoo
- Car seat – some hospitals won't let you leave with your baby unless you take your car seat into the hospital

Now, we have baby sorted, *but what you?* You should certainly pack a bag for yourself too. Being a labor and birthing partner isn't easy – it can be long and difficult. You might need:

- Healthy snacks – granola bars or crackers are great to keep you going as you need to stay energized too
- Don't forget your water bottle – you need to keep yourself hydrated too so take a water bottle or other bottled drinks
- Medication – if you take any regular medication or suffer from migraines, or a sore back or neck, you may need to take medications with you
- Toiletries – you may want to take some shower gel, deodorant, hand sanitizer, a toothbrush and toothpaste, and breath mints maybe. You can take anything that helps you freshen up
- Small bills and loose change – you should have some cash on hand for vending machines or the parking meter
- Cell phone charging cables – make sure they are extra long and don't forget your phone on the day!

- Electronics – you may choose to take a tablet or e-reader, or even a camera to entertain you over this time. If you do, don't forget the chargers.
- Clothing – there's no harm in taking a fresh set of clothes to change into just in case you're there longer than anticipated
- Pillow and blanket – many hospitals don't provide such things for partners, so there's no harm in being prepared with a few home comforts
- Pregnancy-friendly massage oil – labor is painful and long, so take along some massage oil. It can help relax her, and especially soothing if you massage the lower-back area
- A push present for her – some of us like to present her with a gift, right after the birth to mark the occasion. It gives you the chance to show her your appreciation and your love at this wonderful time

Month Seven To-Do List

You've had a lot of lists already in this chapter, so you mustn't feel bogged down by all the things you have to do. We'll make your list this month as simple as possible.

- Please encourage her to take those prenatal vitamins everyday
- Make sure you discuss getting the bags ready for mom, baby, and you, and have them packed by the end of the month (see section above so you know exactly what you all need)
- Ensure your car is filled up with gas as you may need to leave for the hospital at a moment's notice

- Practice using your baby gear before baby arrives – this means using the stroller, folding it, and unfolding it. Also, practice putting the car seat in the car and attaching it safely
- Prepare some postpartum meals and start to stock your freezer with some simple labeled meals, to make things easier following the birth
- She may start suffering from some of the symptoms below:
  - Leg cramps – cramps are normal, due to the extra weight she's carrying. Encourage her to reduce caffeine and smoking, and drink plenty of water. Meditation, stretching, and massage may also help, as can taking calcium, iron, or magnesium. There's no harm in trying these things to help her get some sleep
  - Changes in her nails – some women experience excessive nail growth throughout pregnancy. They can also become brittle, or show white lines and dots, while others may thicken. This is normal, so just encourage her to keep on top of her nail care. Clip them regularly, use cuticle creams, and ensure she's getting recommended calcium each day. If she needs some advice, book her into the salon, but be sure to let the technician know she's pregnant
  - Bloating and gas – as your baby gets larger, it can cause digestive issues which can result in bloating and gas. Drinking water and exercise can certainly help with this, as can your diet, so make sure you're eating your daily fiber recommended intake (at least)

o Hemorrhoids – hemorrhoids can become uncomfortable. They are simply swollen blood vessels in the pelvic area that cause light bleeding. Finding blood in her stool can be scary for her, so it's a good idea to speak to her doctor. She may be constipated. For most people, hemorrhoids disappear if they drink plenty of water, eat high-fiber foods, and stay active. The doctor may be able to prescribe some safe treatments for her too!

o Fatigue – she's carrying extra weight and she's starting to get tired. Encourage healthy eating, drinking plenty of water, and ensure she's getting out for some gentle exercise. All these things can help her get a better sleep, but if this doesn't ease at times, or even gets worse, you could be low in iron, so speak to a medical professional as they want to check iron levels

o Light-headedness – this is common during pregnancy due to her circulation system being under pressure. Encourage her to eat and drink regularly, and she should also ensure she isn't too hot. If this is regular, speak to a healthcare professional

o Growing feet – you can swell in the feet or ankles during pregnancy, and due to the soft bones, her feet may grow. Encourage her to wear comfortable shoes and put her feet up when she's home. Do get this checked out if you're worried, as swelling can be a sign of deep vein thrombosis or pre-eclampsia. It's always best to have this checked out!

- o Leaky breasts – if she's got leaky breasts, this is normal. It could start with small, yellow dots, but it's nothing to worry about. Simply get her some breast pads and encourage her to wear them if she's feeling self-conscious about this, just in case. It may help to have some anyway
- She may also have mood swings, so bear with her, be patient, and help make things as easy as possible by being supportive. Cheer her up when she needs it if you can. Even spending time together watching a comedy or taking a walk can be fun. If you're worried about her mental health, encourage her to visit her doctor and talk about this – you could even go with her
- Your partner will have a birthing plan, so look at it. If you're having a homebirth, have your midwife or doula visit your home to get things ready for labor and delivery

Braxton Hicks Vs The Real Deal

We've touched on Braxton Hicks already, but they are common in the third trimester. Many people, especially when it comes to their first child, struggle to be able to distinguish between Braxton Hicks and real contractions.

This short section will provide you with some key advice.

Braxton Hicks is when the stomach area of the pregnant woman tightens for a few moments, and then relaxes again. The further you get on in your pregnancy, the more intense they can be. They are getting your body ready for labor, and they are nothing to worry about. Typically, you'll get a sole Braxton Hicks, and maybe get another one 20-30 minutes later. Although it feels strange, they're not necessarily painful, but they do increase their intensity as time goes on.

So, how do we tell the difference between Braxton Hicks and the real deal when it comes to labor?

Real contractions start at the top of the uterus, before they travel through the middle, into the lower part. Braxton Hicks, tighten in the abdomen but they tend to focus on one particular area – so they don't travel.

When you're in labor, your contractions do not stop and increase with intensity. Braxton Hicks sometimes reduces the time between the tightening; however, they stop after 30 minutes or so. Your contractions may be Braxton Hicks if they occur in irregular intervals, they are uncomfortable, but not painful and don't get stronger, they taper off after a while or disappear, or if the duration between each one does not lessen. Real contractions are painful, they do become stronger and as time goes on, they last longer without stopping, and the intervals between each one lessen.

Did you know that Braxton Hicks often occur due to dehydration?

Well, this is a fact, so ensure you encourage her to drink plenty. Sometimes a walk and changing your laying or seating position can help. To ease your mind when it comes to contractions, you should follow the 5-1-1 rule:

1.   Your contractions happen every 5 minutes

2. Your contractions each last for at least 60 seconds
3. Your contractions have been going on for over 60 minutes

If this is the case, it's time to call your doctor, midwife, doula, or the hospital.

Top Tip for Dad

She's in her 7th month of pregnancy and you're invited to a party. She's tired, she's emotional, and she's maybe even anxious about the birth. Even though she says she doesn't mind if you have an alcoholic beverage and even offers to drive, there's something she wishes you knew…

Being the only sober person in the room sucks!!!

There's no ignoring that fact. She doesn't want to spoil your fun, so she may not even tell you how irritating it is. You could just have one or two, and stay sober too, but the truth is, she's probably too tired to drive home. If you truly want to be supportive, don't drink and offer to do the driving.

Now, let's move on and talk through some other things you should know. We've put together some common questions, often asked in month 7.

Third Trimester Q&A

You've made it to the third trimester, and you both probably have important questions you want to ask. We've put together three of the most common questions for month 7 and answered them below.

1. She's physically drained, and suffering from shortness of breath, what should she do?

The baby is growing rapidly as she heads into the third trimester, so the best thing for her is to rest when needed, stay hydrated, and avoid standing for too long, or any physical activity that drains her

2. She's had watery discharge, what should she do?

It could be a sign of infection if it's thick, smelly, or discolored, but discharge overall can be normal so it's probably nothing to worry about. Most women get a thick discharge before labor, so keep an eye on it, and consult your doctor if you feel she needs to be checked for labor

3. She has a low-lying placenta. What can we do to ensure the safe delivery of our baby?

If this is the case, there are some measures she should take. She should stay at home and avoid traveling, remain stress-free, in a stress-free environment, and she should also work on her posture. Under these circumstances, it's also recommended that she avoids physical exertion and sexual relations until the baby is born.

Congratulations! You're at the end of the seventh month. It won't be long before your baby will be here. It's time to move on to month

8 next. Just think, in about two months, you'll be holding your new-born…

THE EIGHTH MONTH

She's made it to the eighth month of pregnancy and there's only a short time left. Before you know it, the final month will be upon you both which is why it's so important to prepare well and cherish your time together. As you get into this month, it's important to remember that she's going to get more uncomfortable and tired. Comments such as 'not long yet', 'the real work begins soon', or 'the best is yet to come', are becoming tiresome, and she'll likely have mood swings and be tired. This doesn't mean she's not looking forward to the birth of your child, she's simply exhausted…

In this chapter, we're going to cover what you need to know when it comes to setting up your nursery, as it'll be great if this is set up in time for the baby's arrival – plus it helps you both get excited. We'll also talk about preterm labor, birth, and sex during this stage of pregnancy. But as ever, let's look at month eight's surprising fact.

Incredible Fact #8

If she has heartburn real-bad at the moment and it's regular, *did you know that your baby is more likely to be born with hair?* That's right, the hair on your baby can give mama heartburn.

A small study has been completed that suggests this, however, it's not exactly how you think. It's strange to imagine a baby with a full head of hair growing inside her, no wonder she has heartburn, *right?*

Wrong!

The study suggests it's not the hair itself that causes the heartburn, but the hormones produced that cause it to grow in the first place. Of course, it's important to understand there is some truth in this, we all react in different ways during pregnancy so many women have a baby with hair and have not had heartburn, while others have a baby without hair, but still have heartburn. There are many different causes of heartburn but it's still good for us to dream about what our baby might look like.

Pregnancy Weeks 33-36

As you head into the eighth month, your baby is preparing for birth, so most of the organs are fully formed, baby is putting on weight, and she or he is getting stronger every day. By 33 weeks, your baby is the size of a pineapple – but of course, they're less spikey and are looking much more like a newborn baby. They weigh approximately the weight of a laptop and measure almost 17 inches (or 43 centimeters) long. Their brain and nervous system are fully developed, and their bones are getting harder, except the skull. The skull stays separated and soft at the top until your baby is over 1 year old. This is because having flexibility here makes their journey from your womb and down the birth canal, slightly easier.

Your baby's skin is losing its wrinkled look and is becoming smooth. Due to your baby being bigger now, their ability to move around in the womb will lessen, however, their kicks will be stronger and uncomfortable too – she may be kicked in the ribs or her sides, or other places she's never experienced before. But this is normal!

By 34 weeks, your baby will have layers of fat as it puts on weight, but those layers will help the baby regulate body temperature once they have been born. This helps the baby to fill out and become rounder. Baba's skin will be less red and translucent now, but it is soft and smooth. Your little one has also reached another milestone – their immune system is developing, and she is passing antibodies over. This means that once they are born, they can fight illness. Your baby can also see its first color – this is red! This is because red is the color of her uterus inside.

By 36 weeks, your baby's hearing has sharpened, and they'll recognize your voice and maybe even your favorite songs. Her bump may drop lower, as the baby moves into the pelvis, into the birthing position – with their head down. If your healthcare professional is not sure whether the head is down, they may send you for an ultrasound or an internal exam.

While baby is developing well, their digestion system is still developing at this stage and this won't be completely mature until after the baby is born. Their weight gain accelerates further – it could be increasing by around one ounce each day, but again, this is to help them get ready for birth.

Within the womb, your baby is shedding most of its body hair, along with a waxy substance that's been protecting their skin. This is called vernix caseosa, and your baby will swallow these substances which results in your baby forming meconium – this will show in the first bowel movements they have once they've been born.

I always remember my wife's friend telling us about the meconium, as nobody told her about it. Her daughter was born late at night, and she was taken to spend the night in a hospital ward. Her baby was twisting, so she offered a feed, but decided to change her nappy too. Imagine her surprise when she opened the nappy to find a sticky, brown substance inside… In a panic, she dashed around searching for a nurse or midwife to help. She believed something was wrong with her newborn, so she was in quite a frenzy, but staff were minimal, and the hospital had low lights, as it was nighttime. Once she found someone, they were able to calm her down and explain this is normal. She now tells as many people as possible, so they're prepared for this!

By the end of this month, your baby is as big as a bunch of kale. They weigh around 6 pounds (or 2.7 kilograms) now and are between 17-18 inches (or 46-48 centimeters) long.

They'll be here soon, and once you get to the end of month 8, can you believe there will only be 4 weeks left?

Setting Up the Nursery

Is it that time already? Yes, it's time to set up your nursery and if this is your first child, you may not even know where to begin, but it's not that complicated. We're here to give you the support you need to get that nursery set up.

To set up a basic nursery, there are five things most people go for. They include:

- A crib – for baba to sleep in
- A changing table – to store all your changing equipment
- A dresser – for baby's clothes
- A closet – for more baby clothes, including coats and covers
- A rocking chair – a comfortable place for mama to sit and nurse baby

When buying your nursery furniture, it's up to you how much you spend on those things but it's best to go for neutral colors if possible. Many people buy preloved or are given items from family members, while others upcycle furniture too – just ensure that anything you use to upcycle is safe for your baby. Having a good level of storage is important, and it also allows you to organize your baby 'things' better too. Try not to go overboard, less is more!

Setting up your nursery isn't just about furniture, as many people want to decorate and dress the nursery. When decorating, some people choose a theme, but as a base for your nursery, it's good to go for neutral or pastel colors. Choose a soft color palette, and soft-textured items to create the right atmosphere.

The room can then be jazzed up with textiles, stickers, works of art, lighting, toys, rugs, books, and even a mural. But again, don't go overboard. It is recommended that you aim to create a calm environment with softer colors, as if it's over-stimulating, it can prevent the baby from sleeping.

Before you dress the nursery, you should first decorate it and set up your furniture. That means you can then choose some nice, bespoke, or unique, items to add personality to your nursery. Some creative pieces, like:

- A cushion
- Long, blackout curtains
- A couple of books
- A soft toy
- A canvas painting
- Some soft, ambient lights

Can make a positive difference to your nursery setting as they can create harmony while ensuring it's easy maintenance. As we mentioned earlier in this section, storage is extremely important when it comes to designing your nursery. You can use storage boxes to maximize space, and you could even get under-crib storage. Remember, your child may be a newborn at birth, but before you know it, they will have grown out of things they've never even had the opportunity to wear. With that in mind, you'll need to store clothes of various sizes, to keep them constantly clothed – which isn't easy!

It would be great if you could get the nursery ready, with your partner's input of course. Let's move from the nursery, into your bedroom, as we talk about sex in the last couple of months of pregnancy.

Let's Talk About Sex

Mom and dad always have questions about sex because it's not talked about enough and it's one of those subjects that we don't always like to bring up. One of the most common questions asked is if it's even okay to have sex, as it's not always something we're told.

Your baby is protected by amniotic fluid while in the uterus, and the uterus itself is made up of strong muscles. Sex won't impact your pregnancy provided you have not had any problems or complications, such as issues with your placenta or preterm labor. It's best to avoid sex if your amniotic fluid is leaking, if you have vaginal bleeding, if your placenta is covering your cervical opening, if your cervix has started to open, or if you have a previous history of premature birth or preterm labor.

As her bump becomes bigger, she can lose interest in sex, and sex can feel less comfortable. That doesn't mean you can't be intimate as your partner needs you and your support – try kissing, cuddling, and massage. Laying on her back may be uncomfortable, as can laying on her stomach, so you may need to consider this when being intimate. If sex is uncomfortable simply because of her bump, you could try different positions, for example, she could be on top, or you could try rear entry, with her being on all fours – but ensure she has pillows to prop her up. Other people find it more comfortable to stand whilst having sex but use other things to support them whilst they lean, like a table, bed, or wall.

Month Eight To-Do List

Your month eight to-do list is here, and there are quite a few things to consider this month, but we've made it as easy as possible for you.

- Make sure she's still taking those prenatal vitamins. We want her as healthy as possible in time for the birth

- Contact the maternity unit and see if you and your partner can book a visit. This helps you become more familiar with the environment and ensures you know exactly where to go and what to do when labor starts. Don't forget to ask about the policies in the hospital too, to check if there are still any restrictions in place

- Start practicing techniques for labor like breathing exercises and massage. Using controlled breathing techniques can help you manage the pains of labor. The Lamaze method and Bradley method are among the most popular, and you can book classes or watch online tutorial videos to master the techniques. Massage techniques can also help relieve pain – usually circular movements at the bottom of the back can help. Hot water bottles and ice packs can also help.

- You and your partner should also practice different labor positions because some are more comfortable than others. She may wish to kneel, stand, or lay on her back. Sometimes rocking on all fours can relieve the pressure on your back, during a contraction. Find out which ones she wants to consider – knowing the different ones can help throughout the labor

- Stock your home with essentials to ensure you won't run low on the things you need. Having plenty of food, nappies, wipes, toilet roll, toiletries, and cleaning supplies can make life easier for a while, as you settle into your new routine

- Make sure all the baby's clothes and bedding are washed with unscented detergents by the end of the month. They can then be stored firmly away in the nursery, ready for use

- She'll be suffering from some late pregnancy symptoms, and the three most common include:
    - Pregnancy waddle – when our bump gets bigger, women tend to lean back as they walk, and as a result, they often walk with their feet further apart and waddle from side-to-side. This can leave them slightly off balance and certain tasks can become a little more difficult, like bending for instance. Help her out when you can.
    - Varicose veins – they are swollen veins that bulge at the skin's surface. They are usually blue, red, or purple and are caused by the uterus putting pressure on the large vein on the right side of your body. This increases the pressure on the veins in your leg. They can go away after the birth; however, they can be prevented if the pregnant person exercises daily, elevate their feet and legs when resting, and if she stays within the recommended weight range. You should also avoid standing for long periods and crossing your legs and ankles when sitting. Compression stockings can also help. You can buy them over the

counter, or ask your doctor to recommend or pre-scribe some. If her veins feel hard or cord-like or become tender, painful, hot, or red, she should go and see her doctor.

    o   Sleep issues – sleep changes for many women and sleep can become uncomfortable. Many women also develop snoring and sleep apnea during pregnancy, she should keep an eye on these symptoms as they can indicate other health conditions too. Sleep is im-portant, and there are many reasons why she may not be sleeping well. She could even start feeling anxious about the birth, so it's better to try and tackle it early on as it can lead to other problems. Women who de-velop sleep problems in later pregnancy often have longer labors, could need a cesarean section, and are at a higher risk of developing gestational diabetes mellitus. To support her, encourage her to exercise, eat healthily, and relax – there's not long left to go, so remind her how amazing she is!

- Car seat – it's important that you get the right car seat for your baby. You need one suitable for a newborn. This small, portable seat is suitable for babies up to 40 pounds, and it fastens rear-facing. All newborn car seats have a 5-point har-ness, to keep your baby safe. This means the straps cover both shoulders, both sides/underarms, and between the legs. Always ensure that your car seat meets NHTSA standards – it will tell you if it does, as the manufacturer is required to provide this information. Make sure your baby is dressed comfortably, without a jacket or snowsuit as they can become too hot in the car. If it's cold, place blankets over their body, as you can remove them in the car when it warms up. Make sure you read the instructions fully when setting the seat in, and attaching it to your car, and when buckling in your child. Always check that the harness straps are not twisted, but lying flat, and are snug. You should also ensure your baby's head is secure when in the car seat.

- Offer your partner a perineal massage – the perineum is the area between her vagina and bottom and massaging this area can really help prepare her body for the birth, as this muscle needs to be loose so it can stretch. If she's never given birth before this can help, as sometimes this area tears, which is very uncomfortable. She should choose a comfortable position, either sitting or lying down, or even standing with one foot resting on the chair. Make sure you've washed your hands, pop some oil on your fingers and thumbs, and rub on the perineum area. It's recommended that you use vitamin E oil, sunflower oil, grapeseed oil, or coconut oil. Please your thumbs inside the vagina and press firmly into the sides until she feels a stretch. Sometimes this causes a tingling sensation, and that's normal. Massage in a U-shaped motion, moving from the sides of the vagina and downwards towards the perineum, then back up again. Don't overdo it at first, start with a minute, but build up to 5 minutes. She can do this herself, or you can help too. It's recommended you start this from around 34 weeks as studies show, it lessens the pain in that area during birth and post-pregnancy.

- Your labor playlist – it's time to put together the labor playlist we talked about earlier. This can make the birth much more interesting as it can motivate you both, make you happy, increase your determination, or relax you. Create your lists together and consider the different situations that you may want to tackle – *what about funny songs for labor? Or songs that empower women like Beyonce's 'Run the World', Christina Aguilera's 'Fighter', or Little Mix 'Power'.* Make sure you cater to every mood – and if you, as a couple, have a song, add that to your list as there's no reason why you can't be romantic too! You should be aiming for around 10 hours of music, to ensure variety.

- Consider breastfeeding classes – if breastfeeding is being considered, it's a good idea for her to join a breastfeeding class. Breastfeeding can be tiring and lonely, so having help and support from others can change the way a person thinks or feels about it.

Preterm Labor Premature Birth

Preterm labor is when labor occurs before 37 weeks of pregnancy, and many parents worry about this and premature birth at this stage, as the baby isn't quite ready to be born, but this doesn't mean they won't survive.

There are a range of symptoms she may suffer from if she experiences preterm labor. The telltale signs include:

- Backache – lower back ache, either constant or it will come and go. This backache will not ease regardless of what you do

- Contractions – if they occur every 10 minutes or less, and if they quicken or are more painful
- Cramping – menstrual-type cramps occur which can feel like pains of gas or diarrhea, in the lower abdomen
- Fluid leaking from the vaginal area
- Vaginal bleeding
- Increased pressure in the vagina or pelvis
- Flu-like symptoms, including nausea, vomiting, or diarrhea. If you can't tolerate fluids, you should contact your doctor at once

If she is suffering from the symptoms above, it's time to speak to a medical professional. If she's getting regular contractions, it may even be necessary to go to the emergency room, to be assessed by a doctor as soon as possible as a doctor may be able to do all the necessary checks and possibly slow down the labor. If you are diagnosed with preterm labor, you may need treatment, such as:

- Antibiotics
- IV fluids
- Medicine to relax your uterus and stop labor
- Medicine to develop the baby's lungs, rapidly
- Be admitted to hospital so that you can be monitored

Preterm labor can lead to premature birth. One in ten babies born are premature, but this puts them at a higher risk of specific problems in the future. They could develop at a slower rate when it comes to rolling onto their back, grabbing, or grasping objects, talking, and walking. They are also at risk of developing intellectual disabilities, issues with the lungs, cerebral palsy, autism, vision issues, and loss of hearing. Some can also be hyperactive, have emotional outbursts, and struggle in a learning environment. Babies born too early may need neonatal care, and in this case, some struggle to nurse, sleep too much, and can have trouble regulating their body temperature and breathing. They are more prone to other infections too!

There are ways to minimize the risk of preterm labor or premature birth. Studies show that if the mother is able to reduce stress, has good support, does not smoke, and takes good care of their teeth (avoiding gum disease), are often at a higher risk. Those who are overweight, drink alcohol, or use drugs, has other health conditions such as diabetes, blood clotting disorders, preeclampsia, or are pregnant with twins, the risk is also increased. Mothers who are pregnant with a baby who has birth defects, are pregnant due to in vitro fertilization, have a personal history of premature labor, or are pregnant soon after having a baby, are also at risk.

Hormone treatment can also prevent this in some women. Of course, there are some occasions in which it is necessary for baby to be delivered earlier. For example, if a mother has placenta previa, or severe preeclampsia, delivering the baby early could be the safest option. Many people believe that if you are in premature labor, you simply need bed rest, however, studies show this doesn't prevent preterm birth but can cause other issues.

To prevent preterm pregnancy, you should certainly eat healthily and avoid any risky substances. Remember that you should also space out your pregnancies and be cautious with Assisted Reproductive Technology. If you have any other medical conditions, you should manage them effectively, following your doctor's advice, as this too can help you to prevent preterm labor.

What She Wants You to Know!

1. She is starting to get spooked by the birth – even though she wants to be a mother, the thought of birth can be terrifying. Also, they are imagining what life will be like with a little one and be worried in case they fail or if their relationship with you will change. Support her, and let her know you're in this together, and you're in it for the long-haul

2. She's worried you don't find her sexy anymore – when she's in the later stages of pregnancy, her body has been stretched, and bearing the extra weight takes its toll. She's worried about her post-pregnancy body because getting back into shape isn't easy and it certainly isn't the most important thing. Her body has been through so much, so take this into account. You're about to have a child and this child comes first, above anything else. She knows that. But she also knows that after 9 months of hosting another little human, she needs her body to heal, and she may want it to look better. You know her, so tell her she's beautiful, and do things that make her feel attractive. Don't go overboard though – you know your relationship!

3. She doesn't know if she's going to be a good mom and fears failing – having a little one that relies on you is a big responsibility and it's not like they come with an instruction manual, because every baby is different. Once baby is here,

you'll both be surprised by your intuition. Reassure her – she doesn't have to know everything, but you'll figure it out together. Be kind and patient and tell her that nobody knows your child as she does!

4. She's worried you'll feel left out when the baby arrives as baba depends on her all day, every day – you're going to come in second to the baby when it comes to attention, but this doesn't mean she loves you less. Assure her you understand this as your child comes first to you too. Talk about stealing moments together and getting some time together. She doesn't want you to suffer in silence if something is wrong, so be sure to have open conversations – tell her how you feel, and you'll find she opens up too.

5. She's so excited about seeing you with baby – she's waiting for you to hold that little treasure in your arms, kiss baba's head, rock them to sleep, and dote on them. Share in the excitement and talk about her being an amazing mother, and what you're looking forward to when it comes to being a dad. You're both extremely lucky, and so is your baby!

It's Month 8, But What if I Still Have Questions?

Believe me, it's normal to have questions now and post-baby. It's human nature to constantly question everything about pregnancy, birth, and parenthood. You've got at least 18 years from your little one being born, to question every decision or action you take. This is because we want to improve, and we want to make the right choices as parents – there's nothing wrong with that.

Let's consider 3 of the most common questions at 8 months:

1. How do I know if my waters have broken?

When your water breaks, it sometimes goes as a 'gush' which means a gush of water leaves the vagina quickly and it feels odd, as it feels warm. For others, it's a trickle, but it keeps happening and your underwear keeps getting wet as there is regular leakage from the vagina. This suggests your waters have broken. Before this happens, many women pass a mucus plug, which is basically like passing a lump of jello.

2. I'm 8 months pregnant, but why am I so hot?

When you're carrying a baby, you are cooking it to perfection. Your body will reach an internal temperature of 2795 degrees Fahrenheit. No wonder you're so hot!

3. I'm 35 weeks pregnant, and I've been told my baby is breech. Can I still have a natural birth?

Your baby could turn, even this late on in pregnancy, but your midwife or doctor will keep an eye on this and provide you with some advice. They may also discuss your options as if the baby doesn't turn, delivery can be done through a cesarean section, but your midwife will talk through your options and any risks.

You're heading into the ninth month of pregnancy and before you know it, you'll be supporting her in the delivery room.

Eeek – just one month to go peeps!
Are you ready?

THE NINTH MONTH

The final month of pregnancy is here and the birth of your little one isn't far away. There's still so much to learn and do, so in this chapter, we're going to talk about the final few weeks of pregnancy, while also considering some ways to safely encourage labor once your mom is full-term – sometimes, babies get comfortable in the womb and need to be prompted to make their appearance.

We'll also talk through your month nine to-do list as well as discussing when it's time to go to the hospital. While you'll already have a birth plan, we'll talk through some ways you can continue to capture great memories, and we've got some helpful tips for dads, to ensure you're there for your partner as the birth approaches.

The final few weeks of pregnancy can be tiring and slightly stressful – she's relying on you to bring a sense of calm and support her. The most important thing is to enjoy these final few weeks – while you should consider how she's feeling, there's no reason why you also can't be spontaneous too.

Now, it's time to talk about your final, pre-birth incredible fact… This one's certainly mind-blowing!

Incredible Fact #9

Did you know, fetal cells also benefit the mother?

The cells from the fetus migrate to damaged tissues throughout mama's body and repair them. They are still in the body during the cesarean section, and their presence in the wound helps with healing. The cells from the placenta are carried through her blood, into key areas of the body such as the lungs, and wait until they are needed.

That's right, your baby is AMAZING in more ways than you can imagine!

Pregnancy Weeks 37-40

Can you believe it's the last few weeks of pregnancy and by 37 weeks, your baby is the size of a canary melon? At 37 weeks, your baby is still considered early term, but by week 39, they are considered full term. Their lungs are still maturing throughout this month, so the closer they get to 40 weeks, the better. Baby is practicing inhaling and exhaling amniotic fluid so he's using his lungs well and they can, however, still function on their own at this stage – without assistance. Your baby has fabulous fingers, and their dexterity has improved. Baba can grasp his toe or nose, and other smaller objects, and is likely sucking his thumb regularly. This is good feeding practice.

By week 38, most babies weigh up to 7 pounds (over 3 kilograms), and are more than 19 inches (or 48 centimeters) long. Their head is still growing, their fingers and toenails are fully formed, and they are stretching and moving a lot, although they may not kick as much. She can likely feel everything! At 39 weeks baby has reached its birthweight and will typically weigh somewhere between 7-9 pounds (3-4 kilograms) and will be 19-21 inches (48-53 centimeters) long. Their pinkish skin will now be a white color, and baba is ready to make their long-awaited appearance.

When you reach week 40, your baby will be the size of a small pumpkin (the size of a baby) and is waiting for the right time to arrive. They may be comfortable inside mama but will soon be here for you to kiss and hold.

It won't be long now!

Capturing the Moments

We've talked throughout this book about capturing moments, and you should think about capturing moments from the pregnancy, the birth, and just after – in fact, it's something you'll get used to from now on, as you'll want to capture moments throughout the whole of your child's life.

When my friend David and his wife were having their second child, David was obsessed with capturing as many moments as possible and had started to master video creation. He spoke to his wife about videoing the labor, and while at first, she wasn't very keen. She had some concerns about not looking her best and it being a private event, but after they talked about it in-depth and discussed why he thought it was a good idea, she agreed. They agreed it would be private – for their eyes only.

A woman is so busy during labor and delivery, that they don't get to see it for themselves. Sure, you can watch other people's videos, but *what is more precious than the birth of your child?*

Their film was better than expected. As he had clips from throughout the day, from the point she first showed signs of labor, as they set off to the hospital, to the actual birth and the baby's first moments when he was being cleaned and held by his mother. His wife loved seeing her elated husband's face and his amazed face, in anticipation of the birth of their son. Mama was able to see how brave she was, and how she coped with the pain. That's camera gold – stuff you usually don't see!

David took the clips and put together various clips that were amazing to watch. He created some that they could share with the family, but they kept the raw footage too. Filming the birth was a last-minute agreement, but what came from this was such a phenomenal and treasured surprise.

If you capture plenty of moments as images or videos, you can turn them into gifts. You could create a digital slide show, mugs, T-shirts, canvas prints, or even a cushion. You could also create a scrapbook, or create a baby record book.

Photo gifts provide that extra personal touch that helps you create amazing gifts!

Safe Ways to Encourage Labor

Sometimes, baby is a little late being born, and there are some natural things mama can do to encourage natural labor – baby sometimes just needs some encouragement. There are some things you can do:

- Exercise – there are some exercises you can do to bring on labor, naturally. They are:
    - o Engaged breathing – this means you use your core and diaphragm to breathe as you inhale through the nose. Hold in your abdominal muscles and hold your breath, then breathe out through the mouth, slowly. Relax yourself when you exhale and imagine pushing the baby down and out. Your pelvic floor muscles will relax, and you should be able to feel this.
    - o The Butterfly Pose – Yoga is one of the best forms of exercise when you're heavily pregnant. The butterfly pose can be helpful and to do this pose, sit on the floor and keep your knees wide. Put the soles of your feet together and place your hands just under your knees to support yourself. Inhale and sit up tall, so your lower back curves slightly but naturally. As you expand, push your chest forward and as you exhale, lower your chin down, lean back, and make your back rounder. You should repeat this up to 10 times, providing it feels good.
    - o Supported Forward Bend – hold onto something stable or sturdy, like a wall, a solid table, or a counter. Place your legs hip-width apart and hold onto the

support as you bend at the knees. Stretch your hips back and press the tops of your thighs back at the same time. Take long deep breaths and lengthen your spine and expand the back of your pelvis. Move your hips from side to side, but only do this for as long as it feels good.

o Supported Squats – they are another great exercise that helps to stretch the pelvic floor and encourages the baby to move down. Stand with your back against a walk and place your list shoulder-width apart. Point your toes out slightly and bend your knees. Slowly exhale as you descend low – just go to a point that is comfortable for you. Keep your knees pointing out to the side and inhale, as you slowly push back up into the starting position.

o Slow dance with your partner – wrap your arms around the neck of your partner and sway the hips from side to side. Find your rhythm and enjoy This can release hormones in your body that can help you relax and stay calm!

o Use an exercise ball – bouncing gently on an exercise ball can also help the baby move down and induce labor, but you should only do this for a few minutes at a time, throughout the day.

- Sex – sex can induce labor naturally too. Of course, you shouldn't do this unless your doctor has told you that you shouldn't, or you can't.

- Nipple Stimulation – nipple stimulation can also induce labor, but you shouldn't do this if you are having a high-risk pregnancy. Nipple stimulation involves rolling or rubbing the nipples. This releases hormones which help the uterus contract.

- Acupressure – is similar to acupuncture but it involves pressure rather than needles. There are specific pressure points you can put pressure on throughout the body to bring on labor. You should always speak to a health professional before you do this and ask if they feel this is something you should do. The places you should apply pressure are:
  o Spleen 6 Point, on the inside of your leg, just above the ankle bone – use your index finger to apply pressure for a few minutes then take a break before repeating
  o Bladder 60 Point, which is on your foot at the side of the ankle bone, close to the Achilles tendon. Use your thumb to apply pressure to the point and massage for a few minutes
  o Pericardium 8 Point is in the palm of your hand, right in the center. Place your thumb on your hand and apply pressure but be gentle. You can massage for a few seconds.
  o Large Intestine 4 Point is on the back of your hand, at the crease between your thumb and finger. This is the most common acupressure point. Place pressure and massage with your thumb for one minute. Then take at least a little break before you repeat.
  o Bladder 32 Point is at the base of your spine, slightly off center, and is the dimple close to your buttocks. Press firmly into the point and massage for a few

minutes, but make sure you're moving towards the buttock itself.

- Tea – certain teas can also encourage labor. You should try Red Raspberry Leaf Tea and Chamomile Tea, but she should do this only when she's at full term of pregnancy.

If her pregnancy is prolonged and baby is approximately more than 7-10 days overdue, her midwife or doctor may suggest a medical intervention. They'll discuss this with you.

Month Nine To-Do List

You've made it to your month nine checklist, and you've done a great job so far. This month, you should:

- Ensure she's still taking her prenatal vitamins over these last few weeks – this ensures she's fit and healthy for the birth, and that baba is too.

- Continue preparing some easy postpartum meals and ensure your freezer is well-stocked with simple, labeled meals. Soups, sauces (homemade for pasta, vegetable, and meat), pies, curries, mashed potatoes, chilis, and stews all freeze well.

- These last two weeks are tiring and take a toll on your partner. She may start to get some extra symptoms, so let's look at these and how you can help:
  - Lower abdominal pressure – this is likely the baby moving its head into the birth position. She should

complete light exercise, such as walking, but also ensure she's getting plenty of rest time too.

o Decreased appetite – there's not a room in there, so it's likely she won't have much of an appetite. Encourage her to eat little but often, to keep up her energy levels. Having 5 small meals, rather than three larger meals could be beneficial to her. Soups can be great, as you can pack them with vegetables. Treat her to something she fancies too!

o Vaginal discharge or spotting – this can be a sign of heading towards labor, but if she's concerned, it's best to speak to a medical professional about this. Rest can help, along with plenty of water to keep her hydrated.

o Swollen ankles – they are so common, and we've discussed them previously. She should rest with her feet elevated, but she should also participate in ankle exercises, by circling her feet (both ways), and also pointing her toes down, and then up. Repeat a few times, to get your circulation moving.

o Trouble sleeping – this can be worse in the last few weeks as she just won't be comfortable. She should sleep on her side and use pillows to prop her up. Relaxation techniques such as breathing exercises or listening to relaxing music can help too. You should also encourage her to keep exercising, eat healthily, and stay hydrated to the best of her ability, but when it comes to exercise, she should not overdo it. You should also encourage her to take naps during the day if she needs to!

We've kept the to-do list as simple as possible because the birth is happening soon, and you'll be running around, chasing your tail. Dad should also get plenty of rest too, and ensure they are eating healthily and exercising. Mom and baba need you!

It's Go Time!

She's in labor and you've been anticipating this time, however, now the time has arrived, you don't know what to do exactly...

Let's talk about when you should take her to the hospital!

Her doctor or midwife will be able to inform you what to do when she's in labor. You probably need to call the hospital or go directly, but this can differ, depending on your medical history. If you have medical conditions or if you've had complications, your doctor will advise you of what to do.

Generally, she would be advised to go to the hospital once she's in established or active labor. When she goes into labor, her contractions will be consistent and increase over time. There is a general rule to follow called the 5-1-1 rule which means she should go to hospital when her contractions are 5 minutes apart, and each contraction lasts for 1 minute. The final 1 means 1 hour, as her contractions will have been going on for an hour. This is established or active labor. If her contractions feel more painful, last longer than a minute, or the time reduces in between in under an hour, but are consistent, you should go to hospital or at least call the maternity department or clinic to talk about when you should go.

If her water breaks, there's no need to go straight to the hospital unless labor is active. You should call your doctor or midwife for advice, as they may want to examine her. If she has a brown discharge after her waters break, is bleeding, or is having a high-risk pregnancy you should always call your doctor, midwife, or the birthing center for advice. Sometimes, women have a show, which is a plug of mucus discharge, usually streaked with blood and this can signify the start of your labor, however, it can take several days to kick in. For others, it's instant.

If your pregnant partner:

- Starts bleeding (especially if it's red and there's a lot of it)
- Notices that baby isn't as active, so isn't moving as much as it usually does
- Has an increased amount of fluid or discharge (if it's green, brown, or bloody – this is a warning sign)

She should call her doctor or midwife for advice, immediately. When it comes to your baby, you can't be too careful. If any of these symptoms or active labor starts preterm, you should seek medical attention as soon as possible.

Helpful Tips for Dad

There are some things your partner wants you to know. Being on the same page as her and understanding what she needs or wants can make a difference – it keeps dad in the good books, at least. You need to know that:

- She's worried that breastfeeding will be too difficult – breastfeeding is a huge commitment, and it means that she will have to provide every feed for her baby on her own. Sure, she can express but sometimes, that isn't easy either. You can make a difference in this whole thing, by being her support. If she's up at 4 am crying, hold her. Change the baby's nappy, bathe them, and do some of the things you can do, rather than focusing on what you can't. Encourage her and show her you're there for her and baby.

- She wants you to be spontaneous in the last few weeks – you and your partner will be focusing on the baby once they're here, so for now, you need some time together. Cook her a romantic, candlelit dinner, cozy up on the couch in your pajamas and watch favorite movies, run her a bath, give her a back or foot massage, or create a collage of images from her pregnancy and present it to her.

- If she says she's hungry, she needs feeding now – she needs to keep up her energy levels, so if she says she's hungry, there's no time to mull over what you should eat or where you should eat. It's a case of getting food as quickly as possible before she becomes hangry (a cross between hungry and angry).

Month Nine Q & A – The Lowdown

You're almost there, and that's great, but there are still some questions you may have regarding the final month of pregnancy. We'll cover the most common here:

1. What if her labor comes on too quickly or you leave it too late to visit the hospital?

Simply call 911 and explain. They'll ask you some questions and send medical professionals who are trained to deliver babies safely. They can then check her out and decide whether to deliver at home or take her to the hospital whilst in their care.

2. She's tired all the time. What can she do to overcome such fatigue?

Fatigue is a common symptom late on in pregnancy, but the best thing you can do is stay calm, avoid stress, and do some light exercise. Housework can also be good, but she shouldn't do any heavy lifting. If she needs an extra nap, she should take one and not feel guilty about it.

3. Her due date passed 6 days ago, what should she do?

Contact her doctor or midwife for advice, as they will want to check her out. They can then tell her what's next and how to proceed.

4. Her doctor said that her placenta is 'posterior'. I don't know what this means. Is it harmful for my baby?

A posterior placenta is nothing to worry about. It's simply a reference for the doctor, so they know they know the position of the placenta.

If you or your partner have any remaining questions, don't be afraid to talk to a medical professional. They'll be glad you're asking questions and taking an interest.

Now, it's baby time!

So, let's move on to chapter 10, and talk labor and delivery.

LABOR AND DELIVERY

You've made it! It's time for your little one to be born, and it can't come soon enough for you or her. That's why this chapter talks you through the stages of labor, as well as talking through induced labor and epidurals. If you're not sure how you fit into all of this, this chapter will guide you through it all, so you know exactly what to do.

We'll then focus on the birth and dad's role in all this too. By the end of this chapter, you'll know everything you need to about delivery and labor. Now, you just need to master fatherhood – you got this!

Before we go any further, it's time to share our final weird and wonderful fact with you…

Incredible Fact #10

During pregnancy the placenta is created and born within the woman's body. This is a type of organ. The placenta develops in the uterus and its job is to provide nutrients and oxygen to the baby, while also removing waste products from the baby's blood. It's attached to the baby through the umbilical cord.

While this is a fascinating fact, considering she's growing a full mini-human inside of her, maybe it's not so surprising. When your partner gives birth, she is usually given an injection, so she can deliver the placenta soon after as it needs to be removed from the body.

The Stages of Labor

In the first stage of labor, her contractions begin. Contractions cause the cervix to soften and open, but they usually start irregular. These are Braxton Hicks – we've already covered them in this book so far. When her contractions are regular, her waters break, or her mucus plug passes, it can be a sign of labor or early labor. Early labor can last a few hours, or sometimes, it can last several days. The only thing she can do is keep an eye on this, keep moving as much as possible, and wait for established or active labor to kick in.

If she's concerned or unsure, she should always seek advice – both she and the baby are too important to ignore signs or symptoms, so if she's worried, there's no harm in contacting a healthcare professional for advice.

When active labor kicks in, her contractions will be frequent and intense, and her cervix will begin to dilate up to around 6cm, but for the baby to be delivered, mom needs to be 10 cm dilated. Active labor could last up to 8 hours – in some circumstances it can be more.

You're probably wondering how you can help her during this time. You can't take her pain away, even if you wanted to. You can, however:

- Help to time her contractions, so you know when to go to the hospital, or you can help figure out how her labor is progressing.
- Practice her breathing exercises with her. This will help her focus on the labor and birth and encourage her.
- Help them roll on a birthing ball. Doing this won't be easy for her, but with your support, it can help quicken the labor.
- Take a warm shower with her. This provides you with some intimate time together, and your presence can activate hormones to relax her, and maybe even quicken the birth.
- Encourage her to go for a walk or help her change position. Again, these things can help to distract her and help to quicken the labor. Sometimes, if she says still, early labor slows.
- Give her a gentle massage. It's likely her back, feet, and shoulders will be tense – maybe even her legs. This can help her relax through her contractions, so you should encourage her to practice her breathing whilst you're doing this, to cope with labor pains.
- Distract her. You could watch a movie or listen to music, as they can be good ways to calm and distract her.

The final phase of the first stage of labor will be painful and uncomfortable. She will have contractions every 2-3 minutes, and they will last between 60-90 seconds. Just be there for her, hold her hand, and let her know that she can instruct you on what to do. You're there for her and baba now and always!

The second stage of labor includes birth and pushing. It's time for her to get into her chosen, comfortable position to give birth. She may want to kneel, squat, lie on her side, sit, lie on her back, kneel on all fours, or stand. By this time, she'll be fully dilated, which means her baby will move into the birth canal and at this time, she'll be ready to start pushing.

When it's time to push, her body will let her know (unless she's had an epidural), and many women describe this as feeling like they need a poo. She can push through her contractions when she gets the urge. She should use her breathing to do this. One big inhale as the contraction begins, exhale through the contraction, and little pants in between. You're her birthing partner, so you can support her and it's likely her midwife or doctor will be there to assist too.

If this is her first baby, this stage shouldn't last any longer than 3 hours, but if you've already had a baby, it should take less than 2 hours. If your baby is in the right position, the mother delivers the headfirst, and this is the biggest part. The body then follows with further contractions.

When your baby is born, the third stage of labor occurs. Her womb contracts and the placenta is delivered. This generally happens actively, which means she has an injection of the hormone oxytocin into her thigh, which makes the womb contract, and she then delivers the placenta. If she has no treatment, the placenta is delivered naturally, but there are situations when this is not recommended.

Induced Labor

Sometimes labor needs to be helped along. This could be because:

- You're more than a week past your due date
- Your water breaks, but contractions have not begun
- Your amniotic fluid is low around the baby
- There is an infection in their uterus
- You have a medical condition such as diabetes, obesity, or kidney disease
- Your fetus has stopped growing at the expected rate
- Her placenta has separated from the uterus, prior to delivery

In such instances, a medical professional may suggest inducing labor, but this doesn't come without risk. Some inductions fail, while others reduce the baby's heart rate. Induction can cause a uterine rupture, or bleeding too. This is only effective if the baby is in the correct position.

If she is going to be induced, a medical professional will discuss this with you both and you will have the opportunity to answer any questions.

Epidural

A common method of pain relief is an epidural, and it helps her to manage labor pains. It's a type of anesthesia that relieves pain, but it doesn't block out all sensations. It goes in through the spine, and many women find this effective.

If an epidural appeals to her, she should talk to her doctor or midwife about this and other pain relief options that are available for her when she's in labor.

The Birth

We've discussed a little about the birth already, but it's important to discuss some options when it comes to birth. You and your partner can decide to have a hospital birth or a home birth. We'll also talk a little about C-sections here, as sometimes this is necessary and so far, this chapter has focused on a natural delivery.

Many women opt for a hospital delivery because they feel safer within a medical environment. Being in hospital has many advantages, for instance:

- Hospital can offer her pain relief options. An epidural, for instance, can only be administered in the hospital
- A hospital has a place for your child if there are any worries or concerns, including a neonatal intensive care unit. This ensures your baby gets the care it needs
- You have a support network at your fingertips to help you and your partner through the labor and birth process. They deliver babies every day, so it provides safety
- If there are complications, all the tools you need are available in the hospital. Sometimes babies get stuck in the birth canal and need guiding, with suction or forceps. Sometimes, if the birth is prolonged, staff are there to provide early intervention and can complete an emergency C-section if need be

A hospital birth isn't all good. It can be stressful for expectant mothers to be in an unfamiliar place, so some women feel more comfortable at home. Sometimes, you are limited when it comes to birthing positions, as there may be fewer resources in the hospital. For example, they may not have access to a birthing ball or if you wanted a water birth, there may be limited facilities if those things are in high demand. While you have access to medical professionals, there are limitations on the number of people allowed in the birthing room. At home, you can have as many family members and friends there for support, as you wish. Your midwife or doula will still clear their schedule and be available for the birth too, so you do have support from someone who knows what they are doing.

Some women decide a home birth would be best. You can discuss this with your midwife when you start to put together your birth plan. To organize this, you should talk through your options with your midwife. She will record this in your notes and explain what you need to do. Typically, a midwife or doula will come to your home and care for you when you're in labor, and they'll talk through the process with you and your partner.

For a home birth, you don't need a lot of equipment. Your midwife will provide you with a birth pack that has everything she needs when it comes to the birth of your child. There are some things you'll need to gather too, such as:

- A plastic sheet
- Old towels or sheets to cover the plastic sheet
- A warm blanket – in case it's cold
- Bin liners for dirty linen and rubbish

- A desk light or torch
- Clean, warm towards for the baby
- Containers in case you're sick during labor
- A portable heater

She also needs everything she would pack if she were going to the hospital. Some people also want a water birth, so if your partner would like one, you need to find out if you can hire one in time for the birth. Her midwife can help you with that.

To create the perfect birth environment, you should create a warm, private, quiet, dark, and safe places to ensure she feels relaxed and secure at home.

There are many benefits of having a home birth, and we've identified seven of these, below:

1. She has control over the experience
2. She can possibly avoid medical interventions, although, sometimes this is necessary
3. She'll give birth in a familiar setting
4. There is less pressure when it comes to medication
5. The care she'll get is much more personalized
6. She gets unlimited skin-to-skin contact with the baby
7. It can be more convenient as you don't have to travel any-where, and this can also cost less

There is a downside to this too. The disadvantages of a home birth include:

1. If there's a complication or emergency, she will need to be transferred to the hospital

2. Births can be messy
3. It's not safe if she already has complications or medical conditions

Her midwife and doctor will always have her best interests at heart, so listen to their advice, as there may be occasions when they recommend a hospital birth. It's important to listen to their reasons why.

Some people have a cesarean section instead of a natural birth. For some people, this is planned, but for others, they are rushed for an emergency due to a complication.

Before a person has a C-section, they need to fast for 6 hours before the surgery – this means no food or drink. Some hospitals suggest a little longer fasting time. Your midwife or doctor will give you a list of what you need to take to the hospital with you, but it won't be much different from your previous hospital packing list. You may need some compression stockings to prevent blood clots. You wear these during your surgery.

If she elects for a cesarean section, the surgery should take between 30-60 minutes, but the whole process can take a few hours. She'll receive anesthetic but she'll be awake through the whole thing and will likely feel some of the tugging involved. The anesthetic you receive is an epidural. There'll be several people in the operating theatre, but you can go in to support your partner, and she'll get to see and hold her baby straight away, after the birth.

Following the C-section, she will be in pain and discomfort. This is normal, and she will need to limit her lifting, bending, and driving following this surgery. Her midwife will check her blood pressure, and her wound, and review how much she is bleeding. Afterwards, she'll need to have both a catheter and drip installed for up to the first 24 hours. She will need to stay in bed for at least 12 hours, and after that, her midwife will help her shower.

It's important that she gets up and move around as much as possible, without overdoing it, as this prevents the risk of blood clots. You should wear compression stockings now too, and some women require blood thinning medication too.

It takes approximately 6 weeks to recover from a C-section, so she may need help and support while she recovers. Everyone is different, so her doctor and midwife will be able to provide you and your partner with information regarding the recovery.

There are occasions when a C-section happens unexpectedly, as an emergency. This will only be suggested if her labor is much longer than expected, or if there are complications that put both your partner and baby at risk. Sometimes:

- Labor doesn't really start
- Labor stalls
- Your baby is not in the right position
- The mother is extremely exhausted and is no longer able to proceed as their health displaces signs of distress
- The umbilical cord becomes tangled
- The mother has a health condition that puts them at risk
- There is a tear in the womb
- There is a problem with the placenta

A C-section will only be suggested by a doctor in an emergency and risks the health and safety of mother and baby. It's done when there are very few options available other than this.

We've concentrated a lot so far on the labor and birth, and you're now in the know, but we must clarify dad's role, next. That way, dad knows exactly what to do when it comes to that stage.

Dad's Role

It's important that you can support your partner as best you can, while also enjoying the whole labor and birth, as it means your little miracle is on the way.

You should:

- Be your partner's voice – they can't get out of bed and make their demands known, so listen to your partner and if they want or don't want something, speak up for them
- Don't take anything personally during the birth, as she may say some things at the moment – she's tired, in pain and possibly hungry. Help her stay calm and breathe through the contractions. Give her something else to focus on
- Ask questions – don't be afraid to ask questions for you and your wife. Even if you've discussed them earlier and just want to clarify some points, it's better to ask if you're unsure of anything. You should also ask your partner questions too about what they want and what they want you to do
- Help her to stay focused and relaxed with the coping techniques you learned earlier in this book – you've learned lots

of coping activities, including deep breathing, meditation, and exercise. Help her do this and offer her a massage if she needs pain relief

- Recognize your limitations – only do the things you feel comfortable doing. The midwife may ask you if you want to participate in lots of weird but wonderful things, such as catching baby on the way out or cutting the baby's umbilical cord. Only do what you're willing to do. A guy I know has a phobia of blood, so they missed most of the birth as the midwife encouraged him to look at the baby's head whilst it was still on its way out of the birth canal. There was blood and lots of fluids, so he passed out and when he woke up, his baby had already arrived, and he had a nasty bump and bruise on his forehead.

- Be there to offer your encouragement – she needs your support, and she needs you to encourage her. Labor is tough, so tell her how great she's doing and ask her what you can do to help – she'll tell you!

Labor and Delivery Q & A

Labor is an unnerving time, but also an exciting time too. Let's talk through some labor and delivery questions that you and your partner may have:

1. Is labor over once she's holding my baby?

No, labor is over once the placenta is delivered following the birth of the baby. Although labor is over at that point, the mother also needs time to recover and heal too.

2. How many people are allowed in the delivery room?

Typically, two people are allowed in the delivery room, but numbers vary depending on what hospital the pregnant person delivers at. Speak to your doctor, midwife, or hospital birthing center to find out what their rules are.

3. What is the fetal monitor and is she expected to wear it during the entire labor?

A fetal monitor is a belt that fastens around your bump and checks the baby is okay during your contractions and labor. It helps to monitor the heart rate of the baby, so if they are distressed in any way, they can keep an eye on the baby. You don't have to wear it all the time, but your midwife may want you to wear it for periods of time, to check for irregularities. This is for the safety of your baby!

4. *How many days does she need to stay in the hospital, following the delivery of the baby?*

This varies as it depends on the labor and complications. Some mothers end up going home on the same day they give birth naturally. If you've had an epidural or a C-section, or if there have been complications, she may need to stay in longer, for monitoring or recovery reasons.

5. *Are there any side effects of an epidural?*

Epidurals are safe, but of course, there are risks that her midwife and doctors will discuss. There are a few side effects following an epidural. She could have a headache, feel sick, vomit, or feel dizzy. Sometimes, her blood pressure drops, or she could lose control of her bladder, but once the epidural wears off, this should return. An epidural does not always block all the pain, so the mother may be offered other pain relief alongside this. She could feel like her skin is itchy, have temporary or permanent nerve damage, or her breathing may slow. Although it is rare, she is also at risk of infection around the skin where the epidural tube has been inserted. With the right care and medical attention, these side effects will pass, usually within 24 hours, but your doctor will be able to guide you on this.

If you have any further questions regarding birth or delivery, your healthcare professionals are there to help and support you and your partner, so don't be afraid to talk to them, if there's anything you are unsure of.

This is an extremely important event in your life, so no question is unworthy of an answer.

Now, we've reached the end of this chapter, likely, your baby is here, and you just got the most important job of your life: Dad.

Congratulations! You're going to be amazing!

CONCLUSION

What a journey we've had over the last nine months as we learned about pregnancy and birth and went on a father's journey together. It's been an adventure tackling every month, exploring baby's development, learning about mom's symptoms, and looking at things from a dad's perspective. It's been an honor sharing my experiences and stories with you.

Providing a valuable, practical guide for men is extremely important because labor and birth are not just important for mothers, it's important for fathers too, but not in the same way. Sometimes, we just need a little help and support, so we can be the best we can be. Nobody tells dads what they must do or how they must act when it comes to pregnancy and birth. By reading this book, you:

- Know what to expect when it comes to pregnancy
- Know how to help your partner through every stage
- Are now able to help the process run smoothly
- Can strengthen your relationships

And with this in mind, you now have the tools and knowledge to 100% be there for her!

Most pregnancy books are aimed at women, but as men who don't experience pregnancy first-hand, we must understand how to support expectant mothers, in the way we should, but until somebody shared insights with us on how to do this, we could not be as impactful. Until now!

Sharing in the birth of your child is an experience you'll never forget, so you should embrace it and make the most of it, just as this book instructs you. You no longer must sit on the sidelines, hoping you know what to do because this book has told you exactly what to do.

We've been on an incredible journey together and you're certainly ready for fatherhood. You've tackled the hospital bag, making means, and along the way you've learned important tips from men who've previously made mistakes, and provided their wisdom so the same does not happen to you.

You're going to be an amazing father, just like you've been an amazing dad-to-be and partner throughout this book.

Get ready – life as you know it is about to change forever.

Now you've read this practical guide, why not head on over to my author page and leave a review? Just click here! [insert link]

Just remember...

Only the best dads let their children fly. Only the most loved children will soar. Thank you for giving me wings."

— UNKNOWN

REFERENCES

https://www.geisinger.org/patient-care/conditions-treatments-specialty/questions-to-ask-during-prenatal-appointments

https://www.whattoexpect.com/pregnancy/pregnancy-health/prenatal-appointments/

https://www.romper.com/life/embeba-soothing-patches-review

https://www.glamour.com/gallery/10-things-hes-thinking-when-you-tell-him-youre-pregnant

https://www.thebump.com/pregnancy-week-by-week/4-weeks-pregnant

https://www.whattoexpect.com/pregnancy/week-by-week/week-3.aspx

https://www.whattoexpect.com/getting-pregnant/ovulation/implantation/#:~:text=Implantation%20is%20a%20process%20that,implantation%20is%20another%20crucial%20hurdle

https://www.ucsfhealth.org/education/conception-how-it-works

https://www.healthline.com/health/womens-health/what-is-ovulation#timing

https://www.goodtherapy.org/blog/couvade-syndrome-when-expectant-dads-get-pregnancy-symptoms-0116197

https://www.nhs.uk/pregnancy/week-by-week/1-to-12/4-weeks/

https://www.mayoclinichealthsystem.org/hometown-health/speaking-of-health/trying-to-get-pregnant-select-a-lubricant-that-is-most-helpful-for-sperm#:~:text=However%2C%20many%20couples%20who%20are,in%20order%20to%20fertilize%20it

https://www.healthline.com/health/does-alcohol-kill-sperm-2#effect-on-male-fertility

https://www.verywellfamily.com/male-fertility-and-smoking-1960256#:~:text=Studies1%EF%BB%BF%20on%20male,and%20increased%20sperm%20DNA%20damage

https://www.womenshealth.com.au/husband-tracking-period/

https://edition.cnn.com/2019/04/25/health/male-infertility-food-drayer

https://www.uchicagomedicine.org/forefront/health-and-wellness-articles/dont-make-the-mistake-of-letting-a-diet-kill-sperm#:~:text=A%20study%20of%20250%20men,ate%20less%20of%20these%20foods

https://www.bupa.com.au/healthlink/family-and-pregnancy/pregnancy/expecting-parent-tips/tips-for-partners/5-things-i-wish-my-partner-knew-when-i-was-pregnant

https://www.smartparents.sg/pregnancy/when-you-are-pregnant/13-things-women-wish-men-knew-about-pregnancy

https://www.midwestfertility.com/5-questions-men-ask-about-fertility/

https://www.fcionline.com/fertility-blog/6-top-questions-about-trying-to-conceive-answered

https://www.tommys.org/pregnancy-information/planning-a-pregnancy/how-to-get-pregnant/questions-about-conception-dads-be

https://www.nhs.uk/pregnancy/keeping-well/drinking-alcohol-while-pregnant/#:~:text=Drinking%20alcohol%20during%20pregnancy%20increases,alcohol%20spectrum%20disorder%20(FASD)

https://www.cdc.gov/pregnancy/features/pregnantdontsmoke.html#:~:text=Smoking%20during%20pregnancy%20can%20cause,800%2D784%2D8669

https://www.romper.com/pregnancy/why-cant-pregnant-women-eat-deli-meat#:~:text=%E2%80%9CThe%20CDC%20recommends%20that%20pregnant,and%20education%20specialist%2C%20tells%20Romper

https://www.cellocheese.com/the-truth-about-eating-cheese-safely-during-pregnancy/#:~:text=Unpasteurized%20cheese%2C%20which%20means%20cheese,are%20made%20from%20pasteurized%20milk

https://www.mayoclinic.org/healthy-lifestyle/pregnancy-week-by-week/expert-answers/pregnancy-and-hot-tubs/faq-20057844#:~:text=Pregnancy%20week%20by%20week&text=Spending%20more%20than%2010%20minutes,have%20fevers%20during%20early%20pregnancy

https://www.pennmedicine.org/news/news-releases/2021/november/moderate-amounts-of-caffeine-not-linked-to-maternal-health-risks#:~:text=The%20American%20College%20of%20Obstetricians,%2Dounce%20cups

https://www.emmasdiary.co.uk/pregnancy-and-birth/1st-trimester-of-pregnancy/can-i-change-the-cat-litter-while-pregnant

https://myhealth.alberta.ca/Health/pages/conditions.aspx?hwid=uf9707

https://www.thebump.com/a/is-it-safe-to-paint-while-pregnant

https://www.artofmanliness.com/living/food-drink/cooking-for-men/

https://www.thebump.com/a/pregnancy-energy-boosters

https://www.goodtherapy.org/blog/8-strategies-for-dealing-with-angry-partner-1206165

https://www.mayoclinic.org/diseases-conditions/morning-sickness/symptoms-causes/syc-20375254#:~:text=Morning%20sickness%20is%20nausea%20and,have%20morning%20sickness%20throughout%20pregnancy

https://www.webmd.com/baby/coping-with-pregnancy-fatigue#:~:text=During%20your%20first%20trimester%2C%20fatigue,body%20can%20wear%20you%20out

https://www.healthline.com/health/pregnancy/breast-pain-pregnancy#:~:text=Breast%20pain%20is%20often%20the,body%20is%20flooding%20with%20hormones

https://americanpregnancy.org/healthy-pregnancy/pregnancy-health-wellness/mood-swings-during-pregnancy/#:~:text=What%20causes%20pregnancy%20mood%20swings,brain%20chemicals%20that%20regulate%20mood

https://parentinghealthybabies.com/ways-reduce-breast-pain-pregnancy/#:~:text=Ways%20to%20Reduce%20Breast%20Pain%20During%20Pregnancy%201,5%205%7D%20Patience.%206%20...%20%28more%20items%29%20

https://www.medicalnewstoday.com/articles/bloating-in-pregnancy

https://www.whattoexpect.com/pregnancy/for-dad/pregnancy-pointers-for-soon-to-be-dads.aspx

https://www.nct.org.uk/pregnancy/dads-be/first-trimester-tips-for-dads-be

https://www.mayoclinic.org/healthy-lifestyle/pregnancy-week-by-week/in-depth/prenatal-vitamins/art-20046945#:~:text=Ideally%2C%20you'll%20begin%20taking,of%20healthy%20red%20blood%20cells

https://www.familyeducation.com/family-life/unique-pressures-21st-century-dad

https://www.daddilife.com/health/wellness/dads-struggle-too-and-its-time-we-talked-about-it/

https://www.frontiersin.org/articles/10.3389/fpubh.2016.00199/full

https://www.momjunction.com/articles/things-all-men-should-know-about-pregnant-women_00328964/

https://www.nhs.uk/start4life/pregnancy/pregnancy-faqs/

https://www.sciencedaily.com/releases/2006/09/060923104930.htm#:~:text=An%20obstetrician%20who%20specializes%20in,to%20both%20height%20and%20twinning

https://www.whattoexpect.com/pregnancy/week-by-week/week-9.aspx

https://www.babycenter.com/pregnancy/week-by-week/9-weeks-pregnant

https://www.whattoexpect.com/pregnancy/week-by-week/week-10.aspx

https://www.babycenter.com/pregnancy/week-by-week/10-weeks-pregnant

https://www.whattoexpect.com/pregnancy/week-by-week/week-12.aspx

https://www.whattoexpect.com/pregnancy/week-by-week/week-13.aspx

https://www.parentclub.scot/articles/common-pregnancy-questions

https://www.whattoexpect.com/pregnancy/maternity-leave#:~:text=Oftentimes%2C%20maternity%20leave%20is%20about,newborn%20or%20adopting%20a%20child

https://www.babycenter.com/pregnancy/your-life/paternity-leave-what-are-the-options-for-dads_8258

http://www.strongbonds.jss.org.au/workers/families/dynamics.html

https://www.thebokee.com/blogs/bokee-blog/navigating-family-dynamics-with-a-newborn

https://ericalayne.co/changing-family-dynamics-adding-baby/

https://goop.com/wellness/parenthood/introducing-a-new-baby-to-older-siblings/

https://www.whattoexpect.com/pregnancy/week-by-week/week-13.aspx

https://www.whattoexpect.com/pregnancy/week-by-week/week-12.aspx

https://www.babycenter.com/pregnancy/week-by-week/10-weeks-pregnant

https://www.whattoexpect.com/pregnancy/week-by-week/week-10.aspx

https://www.babycenter.com/pregnancy/week-by-week/9-weeks-pregnant

https://www.whattoexpect.com/pregnancy/week-by-week/week-9.aspx

https://www.nhs.uk/start4life/pregnancy/week-by-week/2nd-trimester/week-14/#:~:text=Your%20baby%2C%20or%20foetus%2C%20is,won't%20feel%20it%20yet

https://www.babycenter.com/pregnancy/week-by-week/14-weeks-pregnant

https://www.whattoexpect.com/pregnancy/week-by-week/week-15.aspx

https://www.whattoexpect.com/pregnancy/week-by-week/week-16.aspx

https://www.whattoexpect.com/pregnancy/week-by-week/week-17.aspx

https://www.babycenter.com/pregnancy/your-body/i-think-my-feet-have-grown-is-this-possible_9428#:~:text=Pregnancy%20hormones.&text=It's%20worth%20noting%20that%20the,even%20a%20full%20%E2%80%93%20shoe%20size

https://www.webmd.com/baby/guide/exercise-during-pregnancy#091e9c5e80036744-4-9

https://www.whattoexpect.com/pregnancy/exercises-for-pregnant-women#safety

https://www.whattoexpect.com/pregnancy/exercises-for-pregnant-women

https://www.babylist.com/hello-baby/20-week-ultrasound#:~:text=What%20Happens%20During%20the%2020-Week%20Ultrasound%3F%20The%20ultrasound,at%20the%20right%20pace%20for%20their%20gestational%20age.

https://www.webmd.com/baby/features/pregnancy-food-cravings

https://www.goodto.com/family/pregnancy/18-pregnancy-cravings-and-what-they-mean-from-chocolate-to-pickles-67916

https://www.pampers.com/en-us/pregnancy/pregnancy-calendar/15-weeks-pregnant

https://parenting.firstcry.com/articles/amazing-pregnancy-quotes-and-sayings-to-keep-you-delighted/

https://uthealthaustin.org/blog/the-most-commonly-searched-questions-about-the-second-trimester-of-pregnancy

https://www.todaysparent.com/pregnancy/pregnancy-by-week/second-trimester/

https://americanpregnancy.org/healthy-pregnancy/is-it-safe/prenatal-massage/

https://www.whattoexpect.com/pregnancy/pregnancy-health/prenatal-massage/#what-is

https://www.healthline.com/health/baby/anatomy-ultrasound#2

https://uthealthaustin.org/blog/the-most-commonly-searched-questions-about-the-second-trimester-of-pregnancy

https://www.todaysparent.com/pregnancy/pregnancy-by-week/second-trimester/

https://www.babymoonguide.com/babymoonFAQ.html

https://www.momjunction.com/articles/things-all-men-should-know-about-pregnant-women_00328964/

https://www.smartparents.sg/pregnancy/when-you-are-pregnant/13-things-women-wish-men-knew-about-pregnancy

https://www.nhs.uk/pregnancy/your-pregnancy-care/20-week-scan/

https://www.whattoexpect.com/pregnancy/pregnancy-health/prenatal-testing-level-two-ultrasound-anatomy-scan/

https://www.healthline.com/health/baby/anatomy-ultrasound#1

https://edit.sundayriley.com/expert-approved-reasons-to-take-a-babymoon/

https://www.healthline.com/health/pregnancy/babymoon#takeaway

https://www.nhs.uk/pregnancy/related-conditions/common-symptoms/swollen-ankles-feet-and-fingers/

https://www.mayoclinic.org/healthy-lifestyle/pregnancy-week-by-week/expert-answers/leg-cramps-during-pregnancy/faq-20057766#:~:text=If%20a%20leg%20cramp%20strikes,muscle%20massage%20also%20might%20help

https://www.pampers.com/en-us/pregnancy/pregnancy-calendar/6-months-pregnant

https://www.nhs.uk/pregnancy/related-conditions/common-symptoms/indigestion-and-heartburn/#:~:text=Indigestion%2C%20also%20called%20heartburn%20or,safe%20to%20take%20in%20pregnancy

https://www.verywellfamily.com/best-baby-registries-4690084

https://www.whattoexpect.com/pregnancy/baby-registry-guides/baby-registry-checklist/#howchoose

https://www.nhs.uk/start4life/pregnancy/week-by-week/2nd-trimester/week-22/#:~:text=Your%20baby%2C%20or%20foetus%2C%20is,breathing%20practice%20in%20your%20womb

https://www.babycenter.com/pregnancy/week-by-week/21-weeks-pregnant

https://www.whattoexpect.com/pregnancy/week-by-week/week-21.aspx

https://www.whattoexpect.com/pregnancy/week-by-week/week-20.aspx

https://www.thebump.com/pregnancy-week-by-week/19-weeks-pregnant

https://www.babycenter.com/pregnancy/week-by-week/18-weeks-pregnant

https://www.healthline.com/health/parenting/baby-born-with-teeth

https://www.whattoexpect.com/pregnancy/week-by-week/week-27.aspx

https://www.whattoexpect.com/pregnancy/week-by-week/week-26.aspx

https://www.whattoexpect.com/pregnancy/week-by-week/week-25.aspx

https://www.babycenter.com/pregnancy/week-by-week/24-weeks-pregnant

https://www.thebump.com/pregnancy-week-by-week/23-weeks-pregnant

https://www.thebump.com/news/pregnancy-lowers-voice-pitch

https://www.babycenter.com/pregnancy/relationships/when-will-my-partner-feel-the-baby-kick_10366574#:~:text=You'll%20probably%20begin%20to,yet%2C%20wait%20a%20few%20weeks

https://www.romper.com/life/oktoberfest-instagram-captions

https://www.whattoexpect.com/toddler/childhood-injuries/infant-cpr.aspx

https://www.webmd.com/baby/childbirth-class-options#091e9c5e80506343-1-2

https://www.parents.com/pregnancy/considering-baby/financing-family/a-nine-month-plan-for-getting-your-familys-finances-in-order-pre-baby/

https://www.pregnancybirthbaby.org.au/braxton-hicks-contractions

https://www.thebump.com/a/creative-baby-gender-reveal-ideas

https://www.thedatingdivas.com/40-unique-gender-reveal-ideas/

https://pursuetoday.com/share-gender-not-name/

https://www.thebump.com/news/pregnancy-lowers-voice-pitch

https://www.premierhealth.com/your-health/articles/women-wisdom-wellness-/3-things-i-wish-my-partner-understood-about-my-pregnancy

https://www.todaysparent.com/pregnancy/pregnancy-by-week/second-trimester/

https://www.romper.com/p/9-questions-to-ask-to-pick-the-perfect-baby-name-5873

https://www.kindercare.com/content-hub/articles/2018/february/baby-shower-games-for-dad

https://www.shutterfly.com/ideas/baby-shower-etiquette/#:~:text=While%20traditional%20baby%20showers%20consist,thank%20guests%20before%20they%20leave

https://www.whattoexpect.com/pregnancy/week-by-week/week-32.aspx

https://www.whattoexpect.com/pregnancy/week-by-week/week-31.aspx

https://www.babycenter.com/pregnancy/week-by-week/30-weeks-pregnant

https://www.whattoexpect.com/pregnancy/week-by-week/week-29.aspx

https://www.babycenter.com/pregnancy/week-by-week/29-weeks-pregnant

https://www.babycenter.com/pregnancy/week-by-week/28-weeks-pregnant

https://www.whattoexpect.com/pregnancy/week-by-week/week-28.aspx

https://www.babycenter.com/pregnancy/week-by-week/27-weeks-pregnant

https://www.mayoclinic.org/diseases-conditions/preeclampsia/symptoms-causes/syc-20355745

https://my.clevelandclinic.org/health/diseases/17952-preeclampsia

https://www.babylist.com/hello-baby/what-to-pack-in-your-hospital-bag

https://www.pampers.com/en-us/pregnancy/giving-birth/article/what-to-pack-in-your-hospital-bag-go-bag-checklist

https://www.verywellfamily.com/dads-hospital-bag-1270763

https://utswmed.org/medblog/braxton-hicks-contractions/#:~:text=Real%20contractions%20start%20at%20the,travel%20through%20the%20whole%20uterus

https://www.momtastic.com/pregnancy/611429-things-wish-husband-knew-pregnancy/

https://swirlster.ndtv.com/wellness-mother/pregnancy-care-25-most-commonly-asked-questions-on-pregnancy-2228007

https://swirlster.ndtv.com/wellness-mother/pregnancy-care-25-most-commonly-asked-questions-on-pregnancy-2228007

https://pregnantchicken.com/10-questions-everyone-googles-in-their-third-trimester/

https://www.whattoexpect.com/pregnancy/week-by-week/week-33.aspx#:~:text=How%20big%20is%20my%20baby,half%20a%20pound%20a%20week

https://healthcare.utah.edu/healthfeed/postings/2016/04/hair_heartburn%20.php

https://www.nhs.uk/start4life/pregnancy/week-by-week/3rd-trimester/week-33/#:~:text=Your%20baby%2C%20or%20foetus%2C%20is,system%20are%20now%20fully%20developed

https://www.babycenter.com/pregnancy/week-by-week/33-weeks-pregnant

https://www.babycenter.com/pregnancy/week-by-week/34-weeks-pregnant

https://www.whattoexpect.com/pregnancy/week-by-week/week-36.aspx

https://www.babycenter.com/pregnancy/week-by-week/36-weeks-pregnant

https://www.verywellfamily.com/setting-up-the-nursery-284580

https://www.thespruce.com/how-to-design-a-nursery-5199207

https://www.whattoexpect.com/first-year/space-saving-tips-for-the-nursery.aspx

https://www.mayoclinic.org/healthy-lifestyle/pregnancy-week-by-week/in-depth/sex-during-pregnancy/art-20045318#:~:text=Is%20it%20OK%20to%20have,preterm%20labor%20or%20placenta%20problems

https://www.todaysparent.com/pregnancy/pregnancy-health/pregnancy-discharge/

https://www.verywellfamily.com/sex-positions-for-pregnancy-2759947

https://www.healthline.com/health/pregnancy/pregnant-sex-positions#overview

https://www.whattoexpect.com/pregnancy/labor-pain/#breathing

https://www.npr.org/sections/health-shots/2016/07/05/484167200/hey-moms-to-be-here-s-what-puts-the-waddle-in-our-walk#:~:text=The%20loosening%20of%20the%20joints,in%20our%20center%20of%20balance

https://www.babycenter.com/pregnancy/your-body/varicose-veins-during-pregnancy_271

https://www.whattoexpect.com/first-year/infant-car-seat-safety#types

https://www.sleepfoundation.org/pregnancy/sleeping-during-3rd-trimester

https://www.bellybelly.com.au/pregnancy/things-pregnant-women-want-their-partners-to-know/

https://www.webmd.com/baby/guide/premature-labor#091e9c5e8000920e-1-3

https://www.mayoclinic.org/diseases-conditions/preterm-labor/symptoms-causes/syc-20376842

https://www.who.int/news-room/fact-sheets/detail/preterm-birth

https://www.acog.org/womens-health/faqs/preterm-labor-and-birth

https://www.marchofdimes.org/signs-and-symptoms-of-preterm-labor-and-what-to-do.aspx

https://www.babycentre.co.uk/a25021594/partners-guide-to-pregnancy-eight-months

https://www.thebump.com/a/good-music-for-labor

https://www.babycentre.co.uk/x1955/what-is-perineal-massage-and-how-is-it-done

https://www.whattoexpect.com/first-year/infant-car-seat-safety#types

https://www.mayoclinic.org/healthy-lifestyle/pregnancy-week-by-week/in-depth/placenta/art-

20044425#:~:text=The%20placenta%20is%20an%20organ,umbilical%20cord%20arises%20from%20it

https://www.bellybelly.com.au/pregnancy/things-pregnant-women-want-their-partners-to-know/

https://www.premierhealth.com/your-health/articles/women-wisdom-wellness-/the-first-look-are-ultrasounds-safe-and-necessary-

https://www.verywellfamily.com/when-should-i-go-to-the-hospital-to-have-my-baby-2759045#toc-when-to-go-to-the-hospital

https://www.healthline.com/health/pregnancy/nipple-stimulation-to-induce-labor#what-the-research-says

https://www.healthline.com/health/pregnancy/acupressure-points-inducing-labor#bladder-32-point

https://www.webmd.com/baby/does-chamomile-tea-induce-labor#:~:text=Chamomile%20tea%20is%20often%20suggested,to%20get%20your%20labor%20started

https://www.healthline.com/health/pregnancy/when-to-go-to-the-hospital-for-labor#:~:text=A%20simple%20rule%20for%20when,for%20at%20least%201%20hour

http://www.uk.momtastic.com/pregnancy/611429-things-wish-husband-knew-pregnancy/

https://news.asu.edu/content/fetal-cells-influence-moms-health-during-pregnancy-%E2%80%94-and-long-after#:~:text=Fetal%20cells%20can%20also%20provide,their%20active%20participation%20in%20healing

https://www.whattoexpect.com/pregnancy/week-by-week/week-37.aspx#section-baby

https://www.babycenter.com/pregnancy/week-by-week/38-weeks-pregnant#baby-development

https://www.whattoexpect.com/pregnancy/week-by-week/week-39.aspx

https://www.babycenter.com/pregnancy/week-by-week/40-weeks-pregnant

https://www.thebump.com/a/exercises-to-help-activate-labor

https://www.momjunction.com/articles/things-all-men-should-know-about-pregnant-women_00328964/

https://swirlster.ndtv.com/wellness-mother/pregnancy-care-25-most-commonly-asked-questions-on-pregnancy-2228007

https://pregnantchicken.com/10-questions-everyone-googles-in-their-third-trimester/

https://family.lovetoknow.com/about-family-values/80-dad-quotes-that-come-from-heart

https://www.nhs.uk/conditions/epidural/side-effects/

https://www.happiestbaby.com/blogs/pregnancy/labor-delivery-questions

https://medlineplus.gov/ency/patientinstructions/000960.htm

https://www.mom365.com/pregnancy/labor-and-delivery/questions-to-ask-during-labor-and-delivery

https://raisingchildren.net.au/pregnancy/pregnancy-for-partners/pregnancy-and-birth/birth-support

https://www.babycentre.co.uk/a1072/dads-10-ways-to-be-the-perfect-birth-partner

https://www.healthline.com/health/pregnancy/emergency-c-section#takeaway

https://raisingchildren.net.au/pregnancy/labour-birth/vaginal-caesarean-birth/planned-caesarean

https://www.babycentre.co.uk/a1028257/creating-the-perfect-environment-for-giving-birth

https://www.medicinenet.com/advantages_and_disadvantages_of_a_hospital_birth/article.htm

https://www.babycentre.co.uk/a1046223/giving-birth-in-hospital

https://fathercraft.com/pregnancy-for-dads-weekly/

https://www.nhs.uk/pregnancy/labour-and-birth/what-happens/the-stages-of-labour-and-birth/